P9-DWU-287

IRISH MARRIAGE– HOW ARE YOU!

by

NUALA FENNELL

THE MERCIER PRESS
DUBLIN and CORK

THE MERCIER PRESS LIMITED
4 Bridge Street, Cork
25 Lower Abbey Street, Dublin 1

© Nuala Fennell, 1974

First Published 1974
ISBN 0 85342 381 4

APPRECIATION

My appreciation to my co-campaigners, the past and present members of AIM Group, and especially to my husband, Brian, my favourite feminist.

Cahill & Co. Limited, East Wall Road, Dublin 3.

ACKNOWLEDGEMENTS

The following books and reports helped me in my research—

Report of the Commission on the Status of Women
AIM Group Report on Family Maintenance Legislation
Report of Irish National Council on Alcoholics January
1973
Mothers Alone by Dennis Marsden (Pelican)
Marital Breakdown J. Dominian (Pelican)
Death of an Irish Town, John Healy (Mercier)
Broken Marriage Michael Viney (Irish Times publica-
tion)
Free Legal Aid Centres Report December 1972.

The views expressed in this book are the personal views of
the author and the other contributors, and not necessarily
the views of AIM Group. Written permission has been
received from subjects mentioned in the book.

THE CONSTITUTION OF IRELAND

The Family,

Article 41.

1. The State recognises the Family as the natural primary and fundamental unit group of Society, and as a moral institution possessing inalienable and imprescriptible rights, antecedent and superior to all positive law.

2. The State, therefore, guarantees to protect the Family in its constitution and authority, as the necessary basis of social order and as indispensable to the welfare of the Nation and the State.

2. 1. In particular, the State recognises that by her life within the home, woman gives to the State a support without which the common good cannot be achieved.

   2. The State shall, therefore endeavour to ensure that mothers shall not be obliged by economic necessity to engage in labour to the neglect of their duties in the home.

3. 1. The State pledges itself to guard with special care the institution of Marriage, on which the Family is founded, and to protect it against attack.

   2. No law shall be enacted providing for the grant of a dissolution of marriage.

   3. No person whose marriage has been dissolved under the civil law of any other State but is a subsisting valid marriage under the law for the time being in force within the jurisdiction of the Government and Parliament established by this Constitution shall be capable of contracting a valid marriage within that jurisdiction during the lifetime of the other party to the marriage so dissolved.

CONTENTS

PREFACE

Many of the letters from which excerpts have been taken for this book were written to me as a freelance feature writer, but a few of them came from the files of AIM Group, of which I am a founder member.

AIM Group is a Dublin based organisation, set up by a small group of people in January 1972, with the specific purpose of tackling some of the problems facing contemporary Irishwomen.

Working on the assumption that legal equality must be the basis of our campaign the organisation isolated and highlighted those areas in which women were both disadvantaged and discriminated against in law, and in which consequent hardship and suffering resulted.

But we also realise that improving the quality of life for women in this county is not just a matter of new laws. Changing public attitudes with regard to traditional prejudices or intolerances where they concern the role or rights of women may, in time prove a greater hurdle for AIM Group than their central objective of legislative change.

AIM Group is the mouthpiece of thousands of Irishwomen who are no longer content with the old order of priorities.

PART I

1:INTRODUCTION

This book was inspired by the many, but specially by the last Irish woman who said to me, 'But I never knew it was like that'. In a sense it wrote itself, I merely linked together comments from hundreds of women who told me what it was really like to have an unstable or broken marriage in this country.

The casualty list is long, and as I hope I will show, the facilities for cure or even prevention are not all they could be. I was defeated in my attempts to professionally categorise the problem areas in marriage as adequately as I would have liked, for the reason that a multiplicity of causes with overlapping effects were present in most examples. For instance brutality, while not being in any way typical of an alcoholic condition was often an attendant factor, and non-maintenance had to be considered both in marriage and in relation to separation or desertion.

Using my own (inexpert) judgement I defined the areas that I saw as the most crucial ones contributing to breakdown in our marriages, but I do not propose that they are the only ones, or that they might not have been aggravated by root causes such as unemployment, bad housing, inadequate education, all of which hit both husband and wife.

The quotations in all cases are genuine, the letters are for real, the problems too. For the purpose of protecting the identity of the writers, I have changed names and facts, irrelevant to the situations, and do not mention the location of any of the writers.

Though I write about marriage disharmony but deal exclusively with the disadvantages from a wife's position, I realise this book would not qualify on a professional level as a sociological survey. Could it perhaps be considered a sociological comment, which of itself might inspire the research so vitally necessary?

For the benefit of the critics who will interpret the

3

emphasis on the wife's problems in marriage as bias, it is important to explain this is in no way intended in a preferential or prejudicial sense. Nor do I subscribe to the belief that all marriage problems are created by men, with women the innocent victims, this would just not be true. The reason the book is based on the wife in marriage, besides the fact that it was women who contacted us, is to illustrate the weak position of a wife and the vulnerability of the children when a marriage fails, to show how unprotected she is under law, and to illustrate how the public by censorious or indifferent attitudes can contribute to the hardship she must endure.

If the chapters read a little like an extended agony column, it is only because women have for years had no other recourse in this country when things went wrong, except to send a letter to the problem columns of a newspaper or women's magazine. It is a form of journalism that creates its own copy, one wonders if the heartbreak letters were to dry up, what would the agony executives turn their talents to? If it was of any therapeutic benefit to a woman to bare the details of her life and marriage to a faceless stranger, there cannot have been much relief for her in an answer that advised prayer and implied that marriage, any marriage is forever.

Many Irish women married a myth. And it in turn was conceived by the male politicians of the 1930s who had a vision of a perfect Irish society, and perfect because it was Irish. We are suffering now from chronically retarded legislation because someone in power saw Irish family life set in a cornfield, the white cottage with turf at the gable end, a submissive and prolific wife, and hordes of rosy cheeked children. That was happiness.

The social and legal climate of today would suggest that there has been more than one visionary amongst the politicians of the last forty years. Only very slowly was it accepted that the mythical quality of Irish life was being strained by modern trends. In recent years we have been taking a long hard look at what we like to call our Christian society. So, if one juggles a few statistics together like our 21% birth rate (England 3½%) 11% admittance to mental

4

hospital (highest in Europe) and 11% of national income spent on liquor, and reflects the family social problems these figures directly or indirectly precipitate, against our under-developed Social Welfare scheme, our inadequate family law, (no divorce), we have a picture of a high percentage of families in various degrees of distress.

Working with AIM Group I quickly discovered that though compassion is a poor substitute for training, it attracted to us many women who would not approach the professionals such as marriage counsellors or social workers, for a variety of reasons. So often are we a clearing house for women with problems, directing them to psychiatrists, solicitors, doctors, that one wonders at the lack of directive and decisiveness in some women. Can it be a side effect of marriage, where one is conditioned 'to depend', or is it merely a symptom of their disillusionment with the establish-ment when problems occur in their marriage? It is remark-able to see the emotional bashing a wife suffers when her marriage goes wrong, her world zooms to the smallest dimension of the kitchen or the bedroom, while her obsession with self guilt, anxiety for the children, concern for the future looms large and uncontrollable. Such women become obsequious, where they may once have been decisive, happy people, their marriage upheavals can reduce them almost to the level of dependent children. This in itself is an indictment of the prevailing trend in marriage of a submissive, dependent wife and a superior, dominant and decision-making husband. Those of us who have been working closely with the distressed wife would say that a state of confusion and inability to cope is a typical pattern, the few exceptions being women who have either retained a measure of independence in their marriage, or have naturally got a resourceful character.

When a wife gets into such a condition that she cannot make decisions, cannot finish sentences, wants to repeat time and again the outrages her husband subjected her to, she can be tedious to any sympathetic listener, which probably explains one of the reasons why solicitors shun women with matrimonial problems. They tend to get a blow by blow account of the conflict, when all they want are the facts.

All many women need is a sounding board to bounce their marriages off, and for that reason we have always been careful to show controlled reaction, either in letters or phone calls to any of the problems with which we are confronted. It would be too simple, if also instinctive, having heard details of the most harrowing and devastating treatment a wife may have endured to advise her to get out of the marriage. Only in exceptionally few cases have we directly advised a woman to leave her husband, in one case because of physical danger to herself and her children from an extremely brutal husband, and on another occasion because of a history of incest.

By and large it would not be easy to influence a woman (even if one wished to), to end a bad marriage. We have noticed that women will endure astounding levels of brutality, indignity, deprivation rather than separate and face the dread of the stigma of failure. Failure in marriage can be rationalised if outward appearances can be retained, but a physical break-up is the ultimate failure because it becomes obvious to all, and indefensible.

If evidence were ever needed to support the ideal of sexual equality in education, training, promotion for the male traditional reasons of 'having to support a family', the plight of the deserted (either physically or emotionally), wife provides it. The ultimate objective should be the extended education of a woman, so that perhaps our daughters may aspire to a marriage freely entered into for the best reasons, and not consider it a conventional inevitability, or an easy mealticket for life.

I do not wish to get bogged down either in the realms of the sociological reasons for marriage failure or in taking swingeing blows at scapegoats, the Church, the Irish Mother or the Frigid Wife.

Readers may however be forcibly struck by some spouses apparent insensitivity to conjugal love, evident in many case histories, which could be significantly responsible for the type of marriage problems we find. An analysis of the reasons for sexual insensitivity and apparent inability to

6

respond to love in the normal way, I must leave to the social researchers.

My function for now is to ask 'Irish Marriage, How are You!'

2:"LIFE A HELL ON EARTH" [ALCOHOLISM]

'It is some consolation to know that I am not the only victim of a bullying, drunken husband, who spends all day in the pub then comes in, makes sure he has a good meal then starts picking on me, terrifies the children, swears, hits and drives me to the point of insanity. I've seen all, but I've yet to see the road with a turning for me, for if I have one peaceful week, the next week life with my husband is like living in a jungle. Should any human being have the right to make our lives a hell on earth? I am never afraid of life after death as it could not be any worse with all the beatings, the naggings I've suffered from my husband. I stick it for my children. I could leave him but my heart would never allow me to desert my dear children'.

This writer's husband was an alcoholic, and women like her are a special kind of martyr, many of them bear out the incisive remark made to me by a member of AA that, 'mostly we pick the right kind of wife'. And in Ireland there are many of the right kind, the women with a high stress point who will not take the easy way out, if even for the reason that she is not sure it will be easy, women who will, with surprising resourcefulness and a handful of sedatives keep family life revolving, keep food on the table, and maybe even the neighbours in ignorance.

It is only fair to say that the wife quoted above had not been attending Al-anon meetings until she contacted us, this to a great degree accounts for the bitterness of her words.

Like a child who knows the truth about Santa Claus but does not want to be seen to believe it, our national attitude to alcoholism is an ambivalent one. Despite the general assessment by social workers and most groups working with family social problems, that alcoholism is the prime factor in

7

marital breakup, child disturbance and a wide area of attendant complaints, little or no social research has been done on the problem. Any that has been carried out deals in the main with the effects of alcoholism on industry, road accidents rates, and the most recent, drinking among teenagers.

True and accurate figures of the number of alcoholics in the country are difficult to assess, by an indirect means it has been established (based on World Health Organisation figures) that we could easily have a maximum figure of 50,000 or 60,000 in the Republic of Ireland. If we further presume that a substantial number of heavy drinkers can be added to this for the purpose of discussing family disharmony, and consider the likelihood that at least half the total number are married men with families, we are talking about a staggering number of women and children who must be disadvantaged because of alcoholism or excessive drinking.

I wish I could say honestly that no woman walks up the aisle with an alcoholic, Irish women do, having reasoned with themselves no doubt that drink is the grubby shirt of bachelorhood, easy to be rid of with new habits. One girl, whose shortsightedness about her husband's bachelor drinking resulted in court cases for non-maintenance, cruelty and finally separation told me quite bluntly that before marriage he had told her, 'no woman is worth giving up the drink for', but the implication is that no woman is worth controlling drink habits for. The desperation of a wife attempting to cope with the problem of an alcoholic husband defies description. Her situation has come about gradually, because alcoholism is a progressive disease, but there is little alleviation of the strain when eventually she, if not her husband, comes to terms with the drinking and realises the truth that he is an alcoholic.

The fundamental behavioural pattern of alcoholics is the same in almost every case, a progressive drop in financial support for the family, loss of sense of proportion about money, and in many cases this is manifested in the purchase of expensive and often unwanted household appliances, seen

8

as an attempt to alleviate guilt feelings. All this in turn leads to an accumulation of debt, often the loss of a job and home.

But the financial problems in the home are only part of the total picture, as one woman wrote, 'We women in this trap do not live as married women, we have more problems than other wives but less real love or affection from our husbands', eventually, the alcoholic's wife lives and suffers in isolation, loyalty to her husband, or indirectly perhaps to herself for her choice of partner evokes a defence of her husband's behaviour in face of criticism from friends or relatives. And they in turn begin to consider her a party to the alcoholism, which in some peculiar way justifies them ostracising her and her children. The high ratio of alcoholics' wives who tell us that their parents, sisters, brothers no longer befriend them reflects the sad lack of understanding and toleration that society shows for the addict and his dependants.

If the number of treatment centres and rehabilitative facilities for the alcoholic spouse can be termed inadequate, his needs appear to be well catered for compared to those of his wife and family.

That universal female panacea for domestic upsets, the chat over a cup of tea, with very few exceptions, just does not hold good for this wife, neighbours don't want to know, relatives are not anxious to be implicated, and others who maybe showed initial interest motivated either by concern or curiosity, eventually lose interest when they discover alcoholism to be an ongoing, recurring problem. 'Don't mention Christianity in a country town. The people here get all dressed up to go to Mass, but they are without kindness, charity or care. I never met such human indifference to the problems around them. They are so cold I feel no touch of kindness. I have no friend here that I could say "I'm miserable, help me".' Such bitter words from a mother of seven children could not have been written for effect, for the same woman wrote of her husband with compassion, 'At times he cannot distinguish between the truth and his lies. It appears that he has to convince himself that we are all wrong

9

to prove he is right himself. The odd thing is that I believe he really cares for the children (and myself) and in spite of all this he cannot help himself. The bigger children realise that he is sick and would be willing to help him if they could. It is a pity too there is no way he could go to seek help, there is not even a Marriage Guidance Council or anything like that in this part of the country'.

There are so many ways in which the children of an alcoholic suffer, directly from deprivation because of misused income, from lack of affection, guidance and from a deep sense of insecurity. Even if they do not witness physical brutality resulting in injury or wanton destruction during violent tempers, they will inevitably be intimidated by the strained relationship between father and mother. Child Guidance Clinics continually see the extended casualties from alcoholism, the sick or emotionally disturbed children, for whom there is some hope of recovery with professional guidance towards adjustment. But for the few who attend Clinics, there must be thousands whose psychiatric problems will not be diagnosed, but which will in time contribute to emotional havoc in their adult lives.

The result of a survey organised by Professor J.N.P. Moore, St Patrick's Hospital involving 400 psychiatric patients disclosed:

(a) That more than one patient in three (36.6%) of those with childhood insecurity have an alcoholic parent.

(b) That an alcoholic parent appeared to be the source of family disharmony in 19% of the whole series.

A devastating trend recurrent in the letters is a situation where sentiments of love and loyalty a child may feel for an alcoholic father are heavily overplayed by a sense of guilt because in everyone else's eyes that father is inadequate or even a social outcast. In at least one situation such mental confusion in a child manifested itself in the son emulating the anti-social ways of the alcoholic father.

His mother wrote, 'I found it necessary to confine myself to my bedroom for the short time my husband was at home, to avoid being called obscene names in front of the children. He encourages my fifteen year old to disrespect me, puts him up to tormenting me as much as possible, and the child does this to please him, much to the horror of the other children. At fifteen my own child throws things at me (to my husband's delight) and makes the lives of the younger children miserable by beating and tormenting them. I know my son loves me too, and is basically very unhappy, he takes little or no interest in his study. For me what is happening is a frightening and terrible thing, but I am powerless to reverse the influence my husband has over this boy'.

Some mothers have to bear the ultimate affliction of discovering that their children too are alcoholics. Another letter said, 'I have been married for twenty-six years to an alcoholic, I have five children, but all of my married years have been agony. Last year while my husband was in hospital having treatment I noticed my son of sixteen (who had just got his Intermediate with honours) was talking and acting peculiarly. He told me he thought he was an alcoholic. My poor boy, always so good, loving and quiet, he had to go away for treatment and was kept in hospital six months. What is to become of him I dread to think. Doctors say he may never go to school again.'

— — — — — —

'I am writing to you in sheer desperation, I am married to a teacher, on a handsome salary with a large farm to boot. He is a complete alcoholic. We have four children six years up to fourteen, but he never gives me a penny. I live on the children's allowance and what I can earn from knitting aran sweaters for tourists. My own family are very good to me. In sheer desperation I approached his manager, the local Parish Priest but he too is an alcoholic, so you can see my position is hopeless'.

Life was more hopeless for this wife than most, for she lived in a small rural town where the traditional facility for 'living on the pass book' did not compensate for the lack of employment opportunities for married women. Heaped on top of the strain about husband, children, public attitudes, an alcoholic's wife has the added stress of going out to work. Only occasionally does the therapeutic benefit to the wife contribute to make the added workload bearable. Mostly the

11

women work at menial uninteresting and poorly paid jobs from dire necessity.

The greatest volume of letters from wives and families of alcoholics dealt with money, where it was either scarce or non-existent and women appeared to complain to a greater extent about their nerves and the need to take pills. All the letters looked for some help, but never money. The significance that we read into this fact is that though women in need thought not in terms of charity but of rights, they were not sure of the extent or substance of their rights.

'My husband gives me no money whatsoever—I have two children eleven and nine. He buys the groceries, and occasionally a bit of meat, but never gives me money to spend, not for clothes, shoes, household goods or day-to-day needs. He has over £40 a week and drinks most of it. Is there no way I can claim some of this for my children? He is always in debt and our medical card has been taken away. They say we are too well off! I had a nervous breakdown, and am supposed to take tablets, but I have no money to buy them, I dread the thought of the children getting sick.'

There are many variations on this theme, but the consequences are the same, a wife who may have been high principled on financial matters before her marriage is dragged down to the poverty line. She cannot even maintain a nutritious diet for her children, but must struggle to keep up external appearances for their sake. She knows that because of her husband's alcoholism, their children must very likely forego an adequate education whatever their intellectual abilities, for grants for higher education are allotted on the income of the father and not on direct social need.

While for a wife and family there is only one real solution to the problem of alcoholism, and that is for the father to go 'on the dry', there are measures that if taken in time would ease some of the hardship. While a system of attachment orders (under which a wife could be paid direct from a husband's pay) would not prevent or cure alcoholism, it would go a long way towards easing the misery it is causing. It is an established fact that alcoholics can hold their jobs,

12

and manage to cope with work conditions despite their addiction. Many reformed heavy drinkers and alcoholics who in the past had showered deprivation on their wives and children, assured us that such a system of attachment of earning would have been a blessing, even if it had not appeared so at the time. Even an apparently insensitive alcoholic suffers from degrees of guilt because of his family's lack of stability, but he is helpless to take effective action.

In the same way, Social Welfare payments, the only source of income for some families should, in circumstances where a father has a drink problem, be paid in part to the wife. In theory this is supposed to be the situation now, but we get letters telling of months of pleading and begging, trailing from one Government Department to another, having to prove the extent of their need to minor officials.

Loss of a home, once if not even more often appears to be an endemic part of life for many of these families. 'The farm is mortgaged to the local Bank, with the Bank Manager chasing him for the repayments. He has made an unsuccessful attempt to mortgage our home here with an Investment Company in Dublin, fortunately I met the valuer before he did and told him the set up'. Too many women have lost the last vestige of security by having the house sold over their heads without their prior notice or consent, and with the ultimate desperate repercussions, for this not to be considered the area of greatest weakness, and greatest need for a re-think. Family homes should be in the joint names of both husband and wife, with dual consent needed for any transaction. Perhaps it is predictable that our greatest cause of marital breakdown should prove to be excessive drinking, for alcohol has always played a very large part in the national scene. In this country attitudes to alcohol can gravitate between the total abstinence policy of the Pioneer Association (which appears to have been relatively ineffective in containing or controlling alcoholism on a national level) and the toleration of even the most offensive alcoholic indulgence. Any private individual disapproval there may be to the abuse of drink is eclipsed by an apparent public tolerance, even at an official level, for instance our lackadasisical approach to drunken driving. There are other countries where alcohol is as much of the national scene, but there can be few places where it is as glorified in drama, or idolised in song and history. With misguided notions of hospitality we still hang on to the system of buying 'rounds', which more than any other factor must set a pattern of immoderate drinking.

One can only assume that the remarkable apathy amongst politicians to tackling this sufficiently documented scourge of our society is prompted by indirect vested interest. If alcoholism among the Irish is to be grappled with realistically, with the control of drink advertising, widespread education on the dangers involved, including a campaign to wean the young away from the pub, all of us will have to be prepared to pay for this change, with an increase in our income tax bill. No doubt the fact that no realistic deterrent, and no serious research into the problem have been put forward in recent times is related to the reality that the sale of liquor and the Duty and Tax derived from it provide a vital source of income to the State. Even motivated by an awareness of the human misery over-indulgence in drink can cause, it would be unrealistic to criticise this inflow to the National Exchequer, if some other comparable substitute cannot be tapped to earn over £70 million now being realised from the sale of alcohol in Ireland.

Nonetheless if we are to continue to reap benefits from the sale of alcohol, we should at least realise our responsibility to the innocent victims who could be called the casualties in the cause of the balance of payments. Out of the millions of pounds should come a substantial fund to support and rehabilitate the alcoholic and his family, and to find out how this can best be done, money should be poured into research dealing with the family of the excessive drinker, for the paltry amounts now being spent are nothing but a meaningless gesture.

3:WIFE-BEATING—A HUSBAND'S PREROGATIVE?

Self-consciously her forefinger went up to a three inch scar beside her mouth. She explained it has been caused by a breadknife. 'If I lock the door he breaks his way in, and physically he is stronger than me. Neighbours cannot always be interfering to help, and short of having a policeman living in I can do nothing. I never refuse him a meal if I have the food in the house, even if it is only a packet of soup and tea. I know he will beat me if he has drink, so I take two sleeping pills and sleep in the bath if he is out late. The bathroom is the only place I can lock myself in. Once after he beat me I had him taken into custody and charged but when leave of appeal was granted and bail fixed, his mother went bailee and got him out. It's not that I am hard but I think jail would have been good for him. Mostly his problem is sexual, I am still a virgin, our marriage was never consummated. When he found intercourse impossible on our honeymoon I thought this would sort itself out with time and patience. It has only become worse and he is tortured by some terrible inadequacy'.

In dealing with the problem of wife brutality, the incidence of which is increasing both in Ireland and England, I am relating the cases as they came to us. Sometimes, as in the foregoing case it is easy to put a finger on a contributory cause of the problem, in later pages a psychiatric view is given.

Canon Law in years past accepted wife-beating as a fair means of keeping a spouse in order, a hundred years ago it was an unquestioned pattern in many families, due in part to the lack of status of a woman, and in part to their chattel value in a marriage.

In all fairness while women can be guilty of precipitating marital breakdown by their infidelity, alcoholism or desertion, when it comes to brutality by and large it is a one-way application, by a husband. One obvious factor to militate against a wife who has to contend with a violent husband is the lack of muscle and might, she is just not his physical equal, nor has she been conditioned or trained as he has been to take a physically offensive position on issues. Because it appears that wife-beating most often shows as an early pattern in marriage (normally passive husbands do not act so out of character) young wives, through shame, ignorance or loyalty, tolerate repeated beatings until they become a way of life for them. Brides are traditionally more romantic than wise.

There is despair and deep unhappiness in many of the letters under this heading, like this mother: 'For twelve years my husband has beaten me, and at the beginning (I was only seventeen when I married) I never questioned his right to do it, but I hated him for it. I was pregnant and had to get married, but that baby was the only one of my children conceived in affection, if not love. The others were a result of rape, and let no one tell me you cannot have that in marriage. My husband is fifteen years older than me and has a good standing in the community, they all think he has a dizzy young wife. For years I tried to tell people how I was suffering, but I only embarrassed them because we have always lived in a country town. Often I wished I could hide one of those self-righteous pillars of the Church in a cupboard in my home, and let them hear a little of our Christian marriage. How I am sane I'll never know. I cannot leave, I have nowhere to go. I have no money and I adore my five children too much to walk out and leave them.' The sister of another victim of such brutality wrote from the country, 'The man has a tempestuous and violent character and I worry for them all, my sister has ten children, with two sets of twins. She is regularly brutally assaulted, and has fled to another sister who lives locally. But he would not allow her to take the younger children and they are very neglected. The husband has in the past been charged with attempted rape of his ten year old, at that time he was warned by the Guards either to emigrate or go for trial, in the meantime with the present undesirable circumstances, no one wants to intervene'.

In so many cases it was a relative or friend who wrote to us, like this mother, 'Unfortunately from the start my daughter's marriage was a disaster. She had courted a boy for five years, and he was always kind, agreeable and appeared devoted to her. He was an only child and totally spoiled. His mother was anxious for the marriage, she thought I would give a big dowry, but I was cautious about giving it on her marriage. In any case she got pregnant straight away and the husband made her life unbearable, forcing her to live with his mother, aged grandfather, and workmen. The mother made her presence felt, she resented my daughter, and criticised everything she did. When she came home with her tiny baby her husband started rough tactics. He caught her by the hair and threatened to choke her, he hit her across the face several times. After one such night she came home to me all black and blue and in a state of nervous collapse. Now I know I must protect her and her child. I can support her, but her husband is saying if he can't kill her one way he will kill her another, as he will take her to the Courts and get the child. He has made no direct approach to his wife to effect reconciliation, apart from sending his Parish Priest over to talk to her'.

According to a Report brought out in 1972 by a group of law students (Free Legal Aid Centres) from their experience there are several recurring factors in marital disharmony, the chief factor seems to be violence, 80% usually brought on by drink. However they do point out that violence and drink are sometimes separate agents. The Report further states, 'The wife in difficulties with her marriage has several options open to her. Sadly none of these provides her with a complete solution to her problem. She may serve her husband with an assault summons if he has beaten her. Most wives are extremely reluctant to take their husbands to court on such a charge. Even when she is persuaded to take the step, there is no guarantee that it will improve her position. A short, often suspended prison term does not always help. In some cases, the husband becomes even more vicious towards the wife after she has taken this step. The Gardai rarely interfere in cases of family dispute.'

Taking a husband to court is a last resort of a woman to get protection. Her position once she gets there is so demoralising that it is conceivable that future beatings would be preferable to legal action involving as it does the exposure to the public gaze of her private life and the flaws in her marriage. Few women away from the relative anonymity of Dublin Courts will bring a charge for assault against their husbands, because it will reliably mean being publicly pilloried, compliments of the local provincial newspaper, the majority of which clear the front page for Court news, and revel in such juicy items as wife brutality, giving the full treatment with names and addresses in their reports.

What women most need when they appear in Court to give evidence of assault is compassion, understanding, even reassurance that they have the right to appeal for protection from the law. What they in fact find is an intimidating line out of male court personnel, who are there to administer the law, not to act as marriage counsellors or social workers, and who all too often appear to interpret the law from the male viewpoint, with bias in favour of the husband in the dock. Not all District Justices lack understanding and patience, when dealing with this particularly sensitive type of case, but I have too often seen how gruff and indifferent certain judges have been in their treatment of the wife as witness.

Many women do not have legal representation, for as has been stated repeatedly in this book, wives have no independent financial means for such luxuries. Because the injuries inflicted must be exhibited in the Court, it is usual for the case to be heard the morning after an assault. The wife may be weak when giving evidence, either from lack of sleep, heavy sedation or the injuries she has received. None of this will contribute to her giving a good representation to the court. If, because she is confused and nervous she mumbles incoherently and the Judge cannot hear her words, he will not always display the necessary patience to extract detailed facts from her. Many of the husbands summoned for wife brutality very obviously need medical treatment, either for alcoholism or other psychiatric illness, but District Justices seldom if ever acknowledge this fact, despite evidence, and it being within their power to detain the defendants for medical examination and report. Normal procedure in wife brutality cases is either a fine or a suspended jail sentence with leave to appeal and bail fixed. I attended court with one wife who had been beaten by her husband only six weeks after he had been given a suspended sentence of six months for attacking her with a carving knife, from which three weeks hospitalisation resulted. The District Justice in question proclaimed the husband to be 'a danger to the community and unfit to walk the streets', then he sentenced him to a year, fixed leave of appeal and a low bail, which was duly paid, and meant this particular 'danger to the community' was free to go.

There can be fewer areas of general frustration for social workers than the situation of violence in the home. The police are reluctant to interfere and much criticism is levelled at them on this count, but can anyone really blame them when it is obvious that a court charade will be the result of their intervention? Very often at some stage between the husband being charged by the police, and the date of the court hearing, a wife will withdraw the charge and refuse to give evidence. It is too easy to put this down to the fickleness of woman, when in a majority of cases it is a result of direct intimidation by the husband. A woman may be too terrified to proceed with legal action, she fears she may not get any protection at the end of it, but merely succeed in stimulating further assaults. She has got to compromise all the time, because he controls the income and owns the house. The simple option for her if she doesn't like the home conditions is to get out.

But can families, particularly wives be protected from violent husbands? Like most problems in marriage this is not a black and white issue on which one can legislate. Many feel that for purposes of legal action, there should not exist the distinction we have at present, where assault within the home is considered in a different context than the same assault in a public place. It must be accepted that women and children are physically weaker than a man, are unable to defend themselves and are in need of protection. Such protection might even be the deterrent factor of a ruling that second time wife assaulters go either to jail, or on medical examination, to a detention clinic for treatment. And in the meantime the families of such violent husbands should be treated as homeless families and accommodation provided until a solution to their problem can be found. This could mean that the wife be reinstated in the family home (regardless of legal title) and the husband debarred until court proceedings define further action. The situation at present is that the husband can remain in comfort in the house, while the wife and children must prevail on friends, relatives, or an institution to take them in, the alternative being to risk further assault, by staying at the house.

Court action for brutality seldom resolves the real problem, but few end as tragically as the case of Ann, a mother of five and four months' pregnant. The morning she appeared in the District Court to give evidence of assault by her husband, she had been up all night, most of it spent sitting in her local police station where she had fled in terror when her husband, who was an alcoholic, had come in at 3 a.m. and attacked her. Charging him was a last resort for Ann. She knew he was dangerous to her, to their five children, and to himself, and she wanted him committed to a detention centre where he could get the treatment she felt he so badly needed.

She asked the judge to remand him in custody for a medical report, pleading that he be referred for treatment. She was told her request was out of order, this was not her privilege. It was implied that she was taking unfair advantage of her husband, who the Judge admitted, 'looks in bad shape and has obviously had a few drinks'. The case was adjourned for a week, the husband freed on his own surety, and over drinks later with friends he admitted that he 'lied to the judge like a gentleman'. But he was dead two days later, having jumped jail, borrowed money and gone to France where he was hit and killed by a lorry. His widow sent the following letter to the District Justice who heard the case:

'On the Sixth of last month I asked you to have my

husband remanded in custody for a medical report due to his illness (alcoholism) that my life was in danger and that he was a danger to himself. You told me that I had no right to make the request even though the guard confirmed my evidence of his previous disposition and convictions for assault. Although I was in a distraught condition (in court) due to the treatment received from my husband, and a total lack of sleep, I endeavoured to make you aware of why I had to take him to court. You gave me little opportunity to inform you of the seriousness of my position. I left the court with the impression that you either did not want to hear my evidence or that you disbelieved me. My sole purpose in being in your court was for the protection of my husband, myself and my children, but within twenty-six hours of your decision, my husband was dead and my worse fears were realised. I write this letter in the interest of people who might in the future find themselves in my predicament. I would now have to carry less worry if you had given me the opportunity of a more patient and less aggressive hearing'.

Any woman who has not been a victim of a beating by her husband must regard the practice with total incomprehension, and wonder how the voluntary contract of marriage with a promise to honour, love and cherish could deteriorate all too quickly to a boot in the ribs or a fist in the eye. We can all surmise about influences that combine to make a wife-beater. In many cases there are strong mother-son relationships, which persist to the extent of the husband's mother showing a total lack of objectivity about his action, and giving him sanctuary or as we have seen going bailee. The surprising thing about such situations is that very often this mother may have suffered beatings from her own husband, but instead of, as one might expect, this giving her a special understanding and compassion for the young wife's ordeal, what appears to happen is that she will justify his behaviour. This type of mother has most likely over the years switched the love and allegiance she might have had for her husband on to her sons, with a consequent critical

21

approach to any daughter-in-law. Another factor many feel could be responsible for brutality in marriage is our educational environment which accepts corporal punishment as a normal penalising procedure.

The psychiatrists to whom I spoke hadn't got a lot to say on the subject of wife brutality, and certainly were not in any way optimistic about a cure. There is apparently a strong aggressive need in men to identify with their traditional place in the family unit. He can have (generally unfounded) fears that for instance, because his wife is on the pill she may be unfaithful, or there may be jealousy of a successful career wife, though this may not be fully revealed. There is as little clinical evidence that wife-beaters are grown-up boyhood bullies, as there is to support the idea that they can be successfully treated and cured.

If a man is made of the stuff in which violence towards a weaker person is part of the behavioural pattern, nothing short of a real religious experience is going to change him. It is worth remembering that some people, like St Paul, who were very violent, were changed through a religious experience.

There are three situations in which wife beating most often occur. They can be identified under the following (a) Provocation (b) Inadequate Man and (c) Problem Sex. Outlined under (a) are wrong attitudes of wives, the ones who nag incessantly and ask for retaliation, the hypercritical wives who don't seem to like anything about their husbands because there was probably not the right basis for the marriage in the first place. Some are dirty, untidy, don't keep house properly nor care for the children adequately, they can be improvident and some even drink to excess.

(b) The Inadequate Man is really an extension of the above, again relating to the wife. This situation, of which wife-beating can be an effect, is created when a husband's worth (as he sees it) is not recognised in his job (there are many good people who are never recognised in their lifetimes). If the wife of such a man does not show sympathy, under-standing and the necessary loyalty to bolster his hurt ego and faltering morale, violent aggression may likely develop in that marriage. In this situation the violent assertion of a man in his home can come about because, whether through lack of influence or lack of ability his aspiration to be boss in his job are not realised.

But (c) Sexual Problems is probably the most common cause. It could be considered a more important factor than the others because it is very often an unknown and unrecognisable one. The amount of impotence and partial impotence one psychiatrist admitted that he comes across is quite astounding. If there is male impotence very often the wife is a living rebuke to the sexual inadequacy and brings out violent frustrations in the man. But the sexual difficulty could be originating from the wife's attitude to sex, her inhibitions, even her frigidity, could in turn make him more aggressive in his treatment of her, if this is his behavioural pattern.

The major linkage with wife-beating found by psychiatrists in this country (and elsewhere) in clinical evidence has been sexual inadequacy or misunderstanding, which leads to masochism and sadism. There is some evidence that a woman may in fact enjoy the pain inflicted by the beatings and in this way get a measure of masochistic pleasure. Psychiatrists do not understand why this should be so, it is a feminine characteristic.

Sex as a main problem area is not so much a result of no formal sexual education, as it is typical of generally repressive public attitudes to things related to sex. Though this situation is changing in Ireland, the changes are not quick enough to cope with other environmental changes and not obvious in a reduction of clinical cases.

Violence is near the surface in most people, both sexes, and any manifestation of violence to-day must be taken in the context of the widespread acceptance of violence all over the world.

Women can be violent also, there are cases of husband bashing, admittedly these instances would not be as numerous, nor would the injuries be as severe as in wife-beating. Women show their aggression in different ways to men, maybe with equal or greater effect to hurt, mentally if not

23

physically. Treatment of a violent husband is not easy, for they will refuse to come for treatment, to be examined or even to discuss the problem with a third party. Will the campaign of equality for women, which one hopes will lead to financial, intellectual, and social benefits for wives, also lead to further conflict in marriage? One would hope not. If it is to become the enriching dimension to married couples that is anticipated, it will need a tremendous amount of readjustment on the part of men towards their wives.

Women are less resistant to change, particularly to the changing roles in marriage, but it means a total re-orientation of a man's place in the traditional group or family, and means an apparent lowering of status for him. Where a woman has a career and is pursuing it in marriage it is only successful if the man is mature and understanding enough to accept her need for equality in this way. Otherwise her job can become a great rival to her husband, and he will be jealous of it and may take this out on her and on the children. Many Irish husbands have not adapted to the equality of women, particularly in sexual behaviour, they don't like the freedom that the pill allows, and though many would themselves consider the occasional extra-marital affaire, they would not allow the same concession to their wives.

Many women tolerate recurrent beatings for years, and suffer emotionally, though they appear to be able to continue functioning, but what one asks are the effects of this home violence on the children?

Predictably, the children must suffer psychologically, whether this is obvious in their young years with behavioural problems, or alternatively, contributes to the perpetuation of the practice of violence in their subsequent marriage with they themselves either inflicting or tolerating beatings. Another effect is that the children can be so desperately afraid of violence that they will become extra timid, even become homosexual because they are so afraid of the aggressive side of men.

Once this trend of beating is set in marriage, it is applied without discretion, even during a wife's pregnancies. As one wife wrote, 'I was beaten and kicked the night before I went in to have my last baby. No one can imagine the indignity of trying to make excuses to a midwife or doctor for black bruises on limbs and abdomen.' Some of the women attribute congenital defects in their babies to violent assaults during pregnancy. One baby was blind, another had an unsightly facial scar, and another was retarded. It doesn't seem possible that a woman can be kicked and beaten all the time of pregnancy and still give birth to a normal child. Though there is no conclusive evidence at present to support the theory, doctors in England believe there is some connection between regular beatings in pregnancy and congenital defects in new babies.

4:"NOT EVEN FIVE PENCE FOR MASS" [MEANNESS]

'Dear Friend,
I'm a married woman with a young family, with little or no freedom. My husband is a fitter with a good wage, but he never gives me any money. I do not know how much he earns, I never see his wage packet, I never get pocket money, not as much as five pence for Mass on Sunday. I am very upset and depressed, is there no law for women's protection from this indignity? Are all just slaves and housekeepers? He does the shopping, I get no new clothes, my clothes are all years old. I cannot give you my name and address', a letter received by me after one television appearance, where I discussed the need for enforceable rights to maintenance in marriage.

The happy medium is achieved in most marriages with regard to maintenance or housekeeping payments, the arrangement most couples operate falls somewhere between the legal minimum of 'basic necessities', and the ideal of total equal sharing. Nonetheless, most wives are financially dependent on their husbands, so what recourse is open to a woman in a situation like the above? Strictly speaking, a wife in this country must desert her spouse if she wishes to take legal action for inadequate maintenance, for a maintenance order cannot be made while they live together, the alternative is grin and bear it. Some District Justices have been known to bend the rules and give a Maintenance Order to a wife presently living with her husband, but the general practice would be to leave the family home first. Even when this order is granted requiring a husband to remit a fixed weekly or monthly amount ot a wife, there is no guarantee that he will continue to meet it.

Welfare and social workers are slow to advise women getting inadequate maintenance to try and take legal action while still living in the family home, for it can often only make a bad situation worse, and does not have even a relative deterrent value. It is generally accepted that if goodwill itself does not exist between husband and wife, legislation to guarantee rights is a poor substitute, nonetheless, a system of attachment orders could go a long way towards protecting the rights of a wife and family to adequate maitnenance. As is the procedure in Holland and other European countries, attachment of earnings means that a Court would have the power to order a husband's employer to pay a percentage of his earnings direct to his family for their support.

Desertion is a term that invokes a physical parting, but it has other meanings for many wives. They are married and cohabiting with their husbands, but deserted in a financial and emotional sense, marriages that exist in name only, with little or no communication, love or respect for each other. Traditionally the Irish family has only one breadwinner, the husband, for Irish wives forsake their careers on marriage and, while this arrangement gives a more secure and happy environment for children in most instances, it establishes a pattern of one earning partner, and one dependent partner. Such a pattern often results in a husband being cast in the superior role and their wife's contribution to the home being downgraded, because she is thought to be motivated by a mixture of instinct and love, and merits no official commercial value whatever on her labour. In the capacity of housekeeper, cook, nurse, teacher, one would think society would evaluate her work as at least equal that of her husband's and protect her interest accordingly. For years Irish wives have been at the mercy of the generosity of the man they married, though he may subsequently have become an alcoholic, a gambler, or turned out to be otherwise irresponsible or plain mean.

Marriage in most cases is one of the most noble of human relationships, but in those marriages where there is financial conflict between a couple, the.wife is far from ennobled, she is put in the most degrading position of any human being. Wherever you turn here, there appears to be a conspiracy to keep women in the kitchen, we have a battle for equal pay, rigid and unfair tax laws on married women, a resistance to creche or nursery facilities on an official level, and female academic establishments where girls are being trained by nuns to believe that motherhood is the highest aspiration for a woman, and marriage the most noble of careers. The non-maintained wife falls between the two stools of having had her earning potential weakened and her rights never clearly established. Seemingly impossible situations of marriage, like a couple not speaking to one another for months or even years at a time, or a husband living in one room of the house like a lodger, are tolerated indefinitely on the assumption that any family background is preferable for the children than a broken home. A mother of six children aged from four to sixteen wrote bitterly, 'Hour after hour, day after day, I do all the work here, and no thanks and no money from my husband. He has nearly £150 a month, his cheque goes from the factory to his bank. I get nothing for myself to buy clothes, tights, lipstick. I have to beg for everything from him, when I ask for fifty pence for a hairdo he says why don't you do it yourself? He pays the electricity bill, groceries, milk, I never handle money. He drinks and smokes forty cigarettes a day, and I often have to stay away from Mass as he won't give me the five pence for the plate.' And more than one wife living in apparent middle class respectability suffers the misery of being treated like a child. 'My husband goes to the supermarket, he decides what we will eat and how much. He pays all the bills, even the milkman, if he is out on a Saturday afternoon, he will not even trust me with the milk money. If my children want a copybook I have to send them to their father, if I want to meet my sister in the city I have to ask him for the bus fare. When I need a coat he prices it, tells me which shop it is in, the colours available and the price and gives me exactly that amount plus my bus fare. It's just a slow form of torture. I don't know any other woman treated as I am, but he sees nothing wrong with it. He thinks he is an excellent husband. Our relationship is very strained, sometimes I hate him. He knows I can't earn anything for myself because of the five chidlren, but how would I be if I left him?'

A surprising number of women whose marital problems stemmed from a husband's scrooge-like tendencies felt it was because their husbands were either jealous, or did not otherwise trust them with the imagined freedom surplus money would give. The prevention of the perpetuation of this type of abuse would only be possible with laws governing a husband's income and property, and the rights of a wife to a portion of both. In the unlikely situation that the wife is the breadwinner, a husband's rights to maintenance should likewise be protected.

Marriage should be an equally based partnership with equal rights to income and home for both parties though they play distinctly different roles in that marriage. In the interest of justice and the protection of a very basic right of a family, such statutory definition should exist.

5:"OFFICIAL STATUS—DESERTED"

'And who ever to this day dares put words on the social evil of the young wife left a prey in a lonely hill home for ten months of the emigrant year? Who dares talk of the practice of the crude chastity belt of pregnancy, which wasn't, in the marriages which followed an all too familiar pattern where a husband came home for the birthing, waiting just long enough to put in the Spring crops, make his wife pregnant again and once again depart.

What kind of society was it which tolerated and by its silence ordained and almost sanctified this two months of the year marriage as being socially and morally acceptable?

There would be sermons on the responsibility of marriage and the duties of marriage and the sanctity of marriage, and there would be no sermons on the joys of marriage'. (John Healy's *The Death of An Irish Town*, Mercier 1967).

Since famine times this pattern of a two month marriage has been a way of life for many. In the strict terms it was not desertion nor was it known as such, at least a tenuous link existed between husband and family, and if over the years it proved strong enough to secure memories in the children and fidelity in the wife, for many it was too weak in later years to rebuild a conventional marriage lasting through every spring, summer, autumn and winter. Too often the two month habitation proved itself to be but a honeymoon, out of total perspective of ordinary married life. When their economic situation allowed life together, many men found they were virtual strangers to their children, and to have too little in common with their wives. The result then in many cases was a last return to England, never to come back.

Ireland has long suffered from the absent husband syndrome, if it sustained the smallholdings of the countryside, it also emotionally crippled the children who grew up on them.

But is the absentee father an Irish phenomenon? It has been an accepted cultural pattern for many rural communities, seen almost as a blessing in the face of extreme poverty, and in the dark days of social indifference, lived with, tolerated, and never seen for the sad malevolent solution that it was. One mother told it this way, 'I was married in 1935, my husband went to England in 1941, but as he was out of work and I was pregnant he came home for the birth of the baby. After that he came home every six months, I got pregnant twice more, and then he wrote and said he had met somebody else. One letter said he was getting a divorce. Then I had a letter from a woman whose daughter he was marrying. I wrote to Scotland Yard, and they brought him home, I can't remember the year but it was springtime. He got four months in jail for not supporting us. After that he sent money for a while, but again stopped sending it. I heard he had a big win on the pools but we got none of it. Only those times I had a good landlady I don't know what I'd have done. I worked on and off sewing, and minding children and cleaning so I could keep my daughters. I heard nothing for years though I wrote to the Salvation Army but they could not find him, and four years ago they said they had closed the case.' Only some of the men who leave their wives to go to England do so with the express intention of deserting. For many it is a genuine attempt to get work, and make a new home and life for their families, but often the combined effects of loneliness, the temptations of a new material world, and very often an accommodating landlady make it difficult to reconcile the two worlds, so in time the new life eclipses the other, and another conscience is rubbed clear, another wife is left on a hillside. Nor is there much evidence that deserting Irish fathers suffer tugs at their heart strings for the children they leave behind. He can always get more, and most do in time.

For the wife there is the disgrace, when the pretence becomes a farce, the deprivation the humiliation to be felt but not indulged in, because for a mother left alone to rear children life is a hard master where emotionalism is unattractive and non-productive.

There are many who believe that the majority of desertions are deliberate in the first instance, marriage and home life have become an illfitting halter, and for those who wish to shrug it off England is an ideal escape hatch. With free access, good employment opportunities in jobs where they need not officially exist, tracing them becomes an almost impossible task. Even in the event of the husbands being located, either by the Salvation Army or the combined efforts of the I.S.P.C.C. and the N.S.P.C.C. only a very small proportion can be persuaded to continue to maintain their families. An officer of the National Society for Prevention of Cruelty to Children in Birmingham said, 'There is nothing so illogical as an Irishman explaining why he won't support his wife. There seems to be something fanciful in his thinking. He'll blame everything and everyone for putting him in the situation he is in'.

With rare guile an Irish husband can avoid the official enquiries, staying one step ahead, as one social worker put it, 'We traced one fellow right all they way up the building of the M1, he was John Murphy, Joe Nolan, Sean Brady, etc. but we never caught him'.

Seldom do men take their children with them when they leave home. This woman's case was an exception, 'I had a very hard life while I lived with my husband. I even signed my home over to him after two years of marriage thinking it would bring peace, but it was a mistake for he sold it and went to England. I am now homeless and would give anything for a room of my own. I became an epileptic when my home got broken up, and I cannot get work. My husband took two of my children to England eight years ago. I want so much to get a legal right to see them without the risk of them being punished by their father. I tried the first year but they were threatened to be put into a home, they got no pocket money if they mentioned my name. I could not keep them for I had no home, no money, but I stopped writing to them for I just could not see them suffer, whatever I suffer myself.'

This is one case where we succeeded in resolving the mother's dilemma, she went to England and in a Divorce settlement got rights to visit her children, but by then they were much older and she herself in deteriorating health.

In October 1970 the Irish government officially recognised the existence of the deserted wife by paying a special allowance to wives and families who can prove desertion. But she must wait (and survive) the qualifying period of six months, originally intended as a test of her resourcefulness to support herself, and make fully sure that the desertion was not short term. In the meantime the deserted wife, while awaiting the qualifying period, applies to the relieving officer for Home Assistance money. She will get little more from him than what will feed her family. Like most officials and civil servants they vary in their personal approach to the human problems on which they are the arbiters. While some are kind and compassionate, others treat those who come to them like criminals.

One mother of two sons, deserted when her children were aged three and seven, which is now over fifteen years ago wrote of her experience with the Home Assistance officer, 'I had to go up to an old falling down school, it was beside a cemetery which I often wished I was lying in, to collect the amount of 32/-. I queued up with the poor people, some of whom were in a very bad state of health. The minute I would enter the room, the Relieving Officer would shout from the top of the room, "Well X, did you hear anything from that husband of yours this week, you can't expect us to continue supporting you while your husband is gallivanting around England".' Home Assistance unlike Deserted Wives Allowance is not a pension, it is paid by the week on the immediate needs of the person and many a woman like the mother quoted cried bitterly when the postman passed by, with no money and no letter for them, because it would have meant not having to face the weekly indignity of begging from the relieving officer.

But not all husbands desert to England. Many wives, whose husbands leave them, but continue to live locally must often wish for the geographic barrier of desertion to England. The collection of maintenance payments in this country, which in theory is possible, in reality is only marginally easier to secure, even through the courts. As everyone knows divorce does not exist in Ireland, and if the husband will not agree to a legal separation agreement, allocating rights to each party, then the wife must live in a kind of matrimonial limbo. Sometimes she will try and hide under the umbrella of respectability by claiming to be a widow, as one deserted wife said, 'In the country where I live I am not supposed to talk about my husband's desertion, I am usually introduced by members of my family, as a widow. You get a peculiar feeling that for part of your life you just did not exist, because people do not want to know about it, or to acknowledge it socially or to talk about it, which is particularly upsetting for me for I have a five year old son, and he is belonging to that part of my life that I am made feel never happened.'

Desertion has no dignity, and leaves a woman without status both in social and legal terms. For purposes of Income Tax she is single, for the Social Welfare means test she is a widow, and to the Catholic Church she will always be a married woman. Like the wife of the alcoholic the greatest frustration and misery of all is caused by the fact that the house in which she lives in most cases belongs to the absent husband. Though she may be working to make the repayments on the mortgage, he can at any time return, reinstate himself in the home, even reassert his connubial rights, and if she does not like this situation, her only option is to leave. As happened to this woman, 'Three years ago my husband left me with two children then aged one year three months and six weeks. He sent me £4 per week through his mother. She in turn would send it to the I.S.P.C.C. Ten months later he returned, and from the time he came back he was rarely at home. He would go off on a Friday and would not return until Sunday or Monday morning. He drank and went with other women, but forced me to sleep with him. I have done all in my power to make something of my marriage as I am only twenty-two. Now he has left me again six months ago, but because the house is in his name I realise he can come back again. I live in dread'. Not all women who could apply the legal sanctions on deserting husbands do so. Many wives who know the whereabouts of their husbands will bitterly tolerate impossible maintenance payments rather than risk the 'disgrace of a Court case'. The fact that they see themselves as the guilty partner reflects the trend of public opinion in most cases. Apparently it is not unusual for friends and neighbours to first query how a wife's behaviour contributed to a husband's desertion, thereby adjudging her guilty. And this tendency towards public adjudication adheres sufficiently to prevent a wife from seeking what relative justice she is entitled to. Unfortunately, this reluctance to take a husband (residing within the jurisdiction) to Court has in the past been a disqualifying factor for Deserted Wives Allowance, as this wife's letter testifies, 'I have been trying to get the deserted wives allowance for the past two years. They won't give it to me. I am a deserted wife for twenty-seven years. They want me to bring my husband to law and I won't do that as my girls are getting married and I don't want to disgrace them by bringing out their father's dirt. It would not be fair to them, we have tried to get along, in that many years he never gave us one penny, God knows I asked him often enough, he just laughed at me.'

And one woman who changed her mind about Court action, 'I will take your advice, take him to Court and chance the publicity. The trouble is he is telling his solicitor he wants to come back and live and support me, but I will not have him. He is right, as I forgave him so many times and each time he cheated. The only reason he wants to come back now is to have a cheap housekeeper and someone to sleep with him when no other woman wants him, but the next woman who looks twice at him and he is gone again.'

Very often a combination of critical public attitudes and the over-sensitivity on the part of a wife contribute to a life of loneliness and isolation.

One mother of two sons, whose husband was untraceable in England, had left her children in the country with her mother to come to the city and work. 'I manage to send £5 a week home for them but it is not enough, though it is all I can afford and still keep myself in my bedsitter. From worry and strain I had a nervous breakdown, now the doctor says I must give up my job and go home to my children. I have applied for the Deserted Wives Allowance, but I could not face to go back home and draw that money from my local post office, as I'm so well known there, it is only a small village and people are inclined to talk about you in my position. Please put "Miss" on my letter when answering, as I am in a flat with single girls who don't know my business'. But in many cases, despite all efforts of priests, friends and even a Court Order, some husbands can downplay their marital responsibilities to family to such an extent that they can actually see their family's deprivation and remain insensitive to it. One poor mother wrote this way, 'My husband left me three months ago and before he went he left me black and blue. I know where he is but no one will make him support us. It is a shame the way a man can just walk out like that. My husband left me on the 6 May, I should have had my period on the 12 May, and it never came, so now I am expecting a baby. I can tell you that I nearly went mad when I found out. My last baby is only one year old and I have eight other children, the eldest fourteen years. I took an overdose of tablets and was pumped out in the hospital and sent home, so I hope you will understand.' And from a young mother of six small children, first widowed and on remarriage subsequently deserted, 'I re-married four years ago, things did not work out well, he was very disappointed I had not a child for him. He was horrible to me and caused me mental distress and I spent three weeks in hospital. He often told me things would be different if I had a child as he wanted a son for his farm, anyway he left me a year ago, and gives us no support. I have not seen him since, he lives about five miles away, he is very well off. He is violent so I would be afraid to approach him, could I write and ask him to support me?'

Though unfaithfulness as a reason for desertion by a husband does not appear to be a regular cause, where there is another woman involved the wives are noticeably more distressed, because this other woman factor in marriage breakup is the culmination of failure, and a form of official statement of the wife's inadequacy, she too becomes tainted by our Irish society's greatest sin, that against sexual morality.

Women in this category tend to be rather self righteous in so far as they will use every opportunity to build themselves up as a perfect mother and wife, and will attempt to support their position be telling you that they went to a pre-marriage course, cooking classes, etc. This sense of guilt over-shadowed by feelings of inadequacy make for a disturbed and very unhappy, even to the point of neurotic, woman. Very often she feels no purpose in life and an inability to cope generally. She needs a lot of help and reassurance in order to face her situation, overcome her bitterness and make her life and the lives of her chidlren meaningful. The danger when infidelity is the cause of desertion, is that the wife will feel personally slighted to such an extent that she will unfairly adversely influence the children's attitude towards the father. She will even if unconsciously, paint an utterly bad picture of the absent father, and any hardship she may be suffering will be used as evidence to support her bias.

Perhaps the indignity would not be so sharp, if there was not deprivation too. This letter is from a mother of four children, whose husband was living in a neighbouring town with another woman, 'I am deserted eight years, I am only thirty-two years old and my whole life is going down the drain. I haven't been outside the door only to Mass in that eight years. It is no life for a young woman, I get so depressed and fed up with life. I am sure the good God did not put us on the earth to bar ourselves in from the world. In a way I would be better off dead than to go on living like this, men in this country should not be let off so light, they are allowed to keep their fancy woman while their legal wife and children suffer. I live on £4 from my husband, it would not keep us in milk!' Another young mother of twenty-eight with great despair wrote, 'I have nobody at all to turn to. In some ways I may be luckier than a lot of women, but that is not keeping me sane. I am exhausted. I am married only three years, with a daughter of two and one of five months. My husband has had girlfriends from the day we married, he is out every night until four or often six o'clock. He has no time for the children either, only if he has an audience and then you would think he was the best husband and father in the world. I used to fight with him over his late hours, but I only got beaten and the furniture broken, so now I don't open my mouth. My whole life is just getting up looking after the children, cooking, cleaning, watching T.V. and back to sleepless nights.'

Lack of scientific research in Ireland prevents me from quoting accurate figures about desertion. One more or less conclusive finding collaborated by social workers, doctors, and a few amateur researchers is that a high percentage of deserted wives to-day were yesterday's pregnant brides, and from this we can draw various deductions.

But there need not be an overture to a desertion. One husband, 'took the weekly shopping list and housekeeping money to get the groceries' and never came back, others have preliminary absences, which condition the wife and family to accepting the final desertion with a sort of relief, because now they know the score and can plan accordingly. Desertion has come a long way from the 'lonely hill home' of John Healy's book, it is a social problem now that crosses all social backgrounds, age groups, and marriage duration. As far as can be established no one type of person becomes a deserted wife.

An observation could be made on the apparent ease with which a father can shrug off his own children, they are the innocent parties whatever guilt can be laid on their mother. One must question the very slender love-link that many Irish fathers appear to have for their own offspring, and be struck at how paltry it appears by comparison with the intensity of the love of the many mothers, who stay in desperately unhappy marriages only for the sake of the children. This is not to say that women never desert their families, some have done so because for the same reasons as the husbands quoted, to get away, to be free of responsibility, but on the whole the ratio is much lower for women.

6:THE GASLIGHT PHENOMENON

A time honoured custom in Ireland for getting rid of unwanted relatives has been the practice of having them committed to a mental hospital. If one were to unfold the lives of some of the longterm inmates of our old rural mental hospitals one would disclose a depressing saga. Small farms and big families in past years created a situation where the acquisition of an extra smallholding by means of having an old unmarried uncle or aunt committed was almost accepted practice. The arrangement was usually lasting, for those who conspired to 'care for' the committed person before the signing over were seldom willing to accept responsibility for them in their senility. Until comparatively recently patients not at all insane could malinger on in mental homes until death, many of them had no one to claim them.

Something on the same theme was the film *Gaslight* shown many years ago, in which Charles Boyer tries to drive his film wife (Ingrid Bergman) mad, in order that he can dispose of her forever to one of the horrific mental institutions of the Victorian era. Of course such behaviour was dismissed as melodrama, until various psychiatrists began to see real life *Gaslight* situations. They discovered the nasty truth that people do try to get rid of spouses by having them committed to mental hospitals.

While there are records of horror-theatre versions of a husband's efforts to convince both his wife and a doctor of her prevailing insanity, the cases of this nature that I have come across, are much less subtle. Whereas divorce is non-existent and legal separation expensive, the laws regarding committal procedures in this country are surprisingly accommodating. While the contemporary situation regarding mental hospital committals may be an improvement on past procedures, there is still sufficient laxity in certain areas, to have contributed to undue misery or even total ruin in the lives of some Irish wives.

According to the *Irish Medical Times* of 20 April 1973, a patient can be committed to a public psychiatric hospital on the word of one doctor (who could be the family doctor). The certification form has to be signed by the receiving doctor at the hospital but under the law he need not see or examine the patient. However, when his signature is on the form, the patient has no right of a second opinion against his or her committal.

Many in the medical profession already feel that there are

loopholes in the present system, one doctor told me that the only one patient he ever committed to a mental home, on the evidence of a near relative, he afterwards discovered to be sane. Since then he has never put his signature to another committal form. Not all doctors unfortunately are so scrupulous.

I pick two specific cases, ones that I have been in a position to check out, and can verify completely. The first mother wrote us, 'I am twenty years married, I have six children. My marriage was never happy but my husband would not grant me a separation. He vented all his spite on me and the children were suffering, he would not let us go but resented maintaining us. Having consulted a solicitor who wrote to him threatening legal action if he did not alter his attitude towards the family, he visited a doctor and told him a pack of lies about me, that I was an alcoholic, which was totally untrue. But he succeeded in having me committed to a home when I was eight months' pregnant, but I was discharged after two hours. Like a fool I gave him another chance, but he persisted in tormenting and even terrifying us.

In desperation I consulted a psychiatrist for help with my husband, and he suggested I ask him to go along to see him. I could never have foreseen what actually happened subsequent to my husband's visit to the doctor. Two mornings later as I was preparing breakfast for the children, my husband came in with two nurses and an ambulance and I was forcibly taken to a mental hospital. I requested to see the doctor in charge, and was told my husband had committed me as a dangerous person, for six months. I begged to go home, but was constantly put off. After two months I was allowed home at weekends, my only weapon then was to play up to my husband, and I begged him to take me out. He agreed, and I was discharged. But by then my nerves were shattered by what he had done, and was at liberty to do again. My husband gloated with triumph and began having affairs openly. He threatened to put me back in the institution if I objected. It is really frightening, and terrible to realise that Irishmen are at liberty to sign their

39

wives into mental homes in order to provide themselves with escape hatches in marriage. Why is it that social workers and those concerned in that field always assume that it is the women who need treatment?'

The second case is rather more horrifying in that the mother involved was committed and discharged repeatedly over a period of a year, apparently on her husband's evidence and the signature of a local doctor.

The reason I can relate this story directly is that, unlike many of the other examples, I had personal involvement in it, and have come to know the mother in question very well.

Her name is Anne, she is forty-four, was married in 1951, and has had twelve children. As with most of the wives in this book, her marriage was at best tolerable, but mostly turbulent.

When she was seven months' pregnant on her twelfth child the first Committal Order was made and she was taken by four mental hospital personnel and retained in an asylum. The order was signed on that and on all other occasions by a local doctor, known to her husband, but not to Anne. He had neither attended, treated nor examined her prior to his visit to sign the committal form. She protested when an attempt was made to inject her—but it was useless, she was approached from behind and given a shot in the arm, then cautioned that if she did not go quietly, the police would be called and would remove her from the house. She was kept at the hospital for one week, and on a Senior Consultant's assessment was allowed home.

Five days after this discharge she was again readmitted on another certificate by the same general practitioner, only to be released again after three days. But a pattern had been established, and Anne found herself, on the expected date of her confinement again in the mental hospital. She pleaded to be taken to a maternity hospital for the birth, so that her baby would not have to live under the stigma of having been born in an asylum. So, under escort, she was transferred to a maternity hospital. She told me, 'I was never insane, but those days prior to the birth of my little girl, I worried for my sanity. I was in an extremely agitated condition, and convinced that the misery I had been through must surely affect my baby'. Memory of this period is the most painful for Anne. After the birth she was discharged by the consultant of the maternity hospital as fit and capable of caring for her baby. Despite this, one week after having arrived home, while bathing her baby, two policemen and the same doctor as before arrived to take her away. She refused to leave the house until the hospital paediatric unit had been notified to come and take the baby in care, and when this had been done at 2 a.m. in the morning, Anne went for her last ride to the mental hospital.

On one occasion, because she rebelled and physically resisted her committal, the police squad car was called and she was taken away as she says 'like a common criminal'. On this occasion her husband left instructions at the hospital that all privileges were to be withheld from her, she was not to be allowed money, phone calls, or visitors and was to be confined to her ward. She was allowed to Mass however, and with borrowed money managed to phone a friend of hers on the way back from the chapel. This friend was a school teacher in one of her children's schools. I spoke to him, 'I was utterly shocked to learn that she was an involuntary patient, I knew her to be certainly sane, rational and an exceptional mother. I was so disturbed by the phone call that I contacted a priest friend of mine who also knew Anne, and we went very soon after to the hospital. We saw the doctor involved with Anne's case, he went to great pains to impress upon us the fact that Anne was not insane or anything like it, that she was merely in the hospital for a rest. My friend the priest pointed out that he knew of more suitable places for a pregnant mother to have a rest. We were not in the best situation to intervene, being neither next-of-kin nor medical people. The doctor was very defensive about our enquiries, and we could do no more for Anne at that time. However, whether as a direct result of our intervention or not, she was released next day'.

When I met Anne, she was living the life of a single woman, renting one room, and working in a factory. She had no contact whatever with her children. As we have seen

41

to be the case before, she had no money to bring a High Court case for Separation, Maintenance and Guardianship of her children, and she felt that even if such litigation were a consideration, her history of mental hospital committals would adversely affect her chances of getting custody of her children. She has lost touch with her baby, whom she hasn't seen since she was two years old, any presents she sends to her children are returned unopened. It would have been too painful for her, and too distressing for the children to use a means of 'gate crashing' in order to see her children. This could not be a permanent arrangement, in the conflict that would have been difficult to avoid, she would have been the intruder, and one with an official record of insanity.

I know Anne as a wonderful resourceful lady, she has made another life, she is generous to a fault, and helps others with their problems, but her own problem she cannot solve. Her children have grown up and away from her, both she and they are the losers in this *gaslight* phenomenon'.

What happened to Charles Boyer and Ingrid Bergman was pure drama, but for Anne the setting was real life.

7: THE MARRIED PENITENT AND CONFESSIONAL PRACTICE

Why does the Catholic Church appear so terribly inadequate in dealing with broken or stressful marriages, when matrimony as a Sacrament is so intrinsically a part of our religion? Many women will bring their marital problems to their priests, this is perhaps because for them the solemnity of the sacrament and the Church ceremony tended to eclipse the legality of the venture, and the legal responsibilities involved in the marraige contract. So, they choose a priest rather than a solicitor when things go wrong, many feel that there must be some spiritual after sales service to go with the sacrament.

But women who resorted in the past to the anonymity of the confessional for advice or solace had a poor hope of practical directive. While many priests show an amazing degree of understanding and compassion with marital problems, many others tend to take the traditional line, and at worse will lecture the wife on her duties and responsibilities and at best will tell her to pray.

It's arguable if celibate pastors could ever have the capacity to mediate or advise on matters relating to marriage difficulties, many of which may be sexual in origin. Many priests actually believe that a marriage which proves to be a 'valley of tears' is better tolerated than broken, in so far as it can be a stepping stone to Heaven, and spiritually more uplifting than a legal separation with relative happiness and contentment. From discussions with various members of the clergy on aspects of broken marriages and the one parent family, it is surprising, certainly to me, to find so many priests who will still consider the moral situation before, and even at the expense of the material, emotional, or legal aspects of the problem family. For instance the majority of priests would most likely advocate the placing of the children of a broken marriage in an institution rather than in the custody of the mother, if there is the merest rumour or hint that she might be involved in any relationship with another man. This, despite the fact that it is widely held by child psychologists than an unsuitable mother, in the generally accepted sense, is far preferable, from the child's developmental aspect, than almost any institution.

To gain an insight into the training a priest gets, particularly where it relates to the area of sexuality and marriage, I asked Fr James Good, who lectures in Medical Ethics at University College, Cork, to elaborate on the subject—

'In the sixteenth century' Fr Good writes, 'the Council of Trent laid down that all mortal sins must be confessed "according to number and species"—that is, the exact type of sin had to be specified along with the number of times it had been committed. From this date Catholic theologians went to great trouble to classify individual sins in order that penitents might comply with this law of the Church. Because of the strong anti-sex prejudice inherited from St Augustine, it was inevitable that sins of married life would be subjected to a particularly detailed analysis with a view to adequate Confession. Consequently it is no surprise when we find that moral theology textbooks descend to the most intimate details when they come to discuss this area.

'What is more important than the attention to detail, however, is the complete absence of a positive theology of marriage in the manuals, and the presence of a thinly-veiled jansenism which reflected Augustine's attitude to sex as a necessary evil in a fallen world. Central to this approach was the assumption that the celibate state was superior to the married state and a consequent downgrading of sexual behaviour even within the sacramental state of Christian marriage. The attitude constantly stated or implied is that the less sex the better, even where it is lawful (which wasn't necessarily very often), and the less pleasure involved in it the better (with the implied suggestion that it would be better still if there were none at all).

'The terminology used in the moral theology manuals was very expressive of this anti-sex mentality. The human body was divided into three areas: the decent parts (those areas believed to have no sexual implications); the less decent parts (those areas with sexual connections but not directly sexual) and the indecent areas (the specifically sexual areas). On the basis of this classification—which physiology and psychology would both staunchly repudiate today—certain moral regulations were drawn up and a code of behaviour was gradually worked out for both single and married life. The permutations and combinations of these terms resulted in a moral code which as times strayed very near the borders of downright pornography. Other terms could be listed to underline the entirely negative approach: *res lubrica* (the slippery affair) was often used as a synonym for sexuality, and *luxuria* or lust was the common term for sexual pleasure whether inside or outside marriage.

'This was the kind of material which the clerical student of the past had to learn as part of his preparation for fulfilling his duties as confessor. The negative attitude towards sex provided by the moral theology textbooks of the day would have been reinforced very strongly by the attitude towards sexuality which he was being given as part of his own personal formation. Celibacy was a pre-condition for ordination, and so as he was seeking to orientate his mind towards a celibate life the clerical student was reinforcing the negative approach to sex that he was learning in his moral theology textbooks. Small wonder, then, that many priests developed strong misogynist tendencies—tendencies which they would carry over into their treatment of women in the confessional and indeed into the whole attitude to sex and marriage.

'The rigour with which many Irish priests confronted sexual problems and situations can be illustrated from many angles. Stories still survive in many areas of the parish priest patrolling the countryside in search of courting couples. J.H. Whyte has documented the anti-dancing campaigns of the nineteen-twenties, some of which lasted almost to the present generation (*Church and State in Modern Ireland*, p.27ff). But it was in the confessional that the real pressure was exercised, for here the threat of refusal of absolution was virtually the equivalent of excommunication.

'Lest we be accused of painting too extreme a picture of priestly attitudes to sex, it may be helpful if we illustrate the common attitude of moral theology textbooks to sexual matters, for it was from these textbooks that students built up their attitudes. Up to very recent times all of these manuals were written in Latin, and even an English manual (like that by Francis Davis) retained Latin for the sections dealing with sex—presumably lest the material fall into lay hands. The most popular manual, Noldin's *Summa Theologiae Moralis*, was entirely in Latin. It is a frightening thought that a Catholic textbook should produce such pure jansenism as late as the nineteen-forties.

'Noldin opens his treatment of marriage by saying that intercourse is an act "which by its very nature was instituted to conserve and propagate the human race". The first section is entitled "The Lawfulness of Intercourse", and the author proceeds immediately to ask himself whether intercourse is lawful—a question on which he expends considerable energy before convincing himself that the affirmative answer is the correct one. Many times in the treatment that follows the reader has to ask himself whether the author really believed this answer to be the correct one. Some of his later decisions would seem to imply that it is not. It is really when he comes to examine "the lawfulness of intercourse in the light of (special) circumstances" that the qualifications come thick and fast. St Thomas Aquinas is quoted to the effect that to seek intercourse to avoid one's own incontinence is a venial sin, as also is the seeking of intercourse for pleasure alone. Only one position for intercourse is lawful, and all other positions must be termed unlawful and venially sinful unless there is a justifying reason for their use. The writers of moral theology textbooks of those days were not to know that the native converts of West Africa were secretly laughing at the nonsense of imposing the "missionary position", as they labelled it, since this so-called natural position was quite unknown to their native culture.

'The jansenistic approach to marital love was nowhere more clear than in the prohibition of sex in proximity to reception of the Eucharist. Relying on St Paul's suggestion that married couples abstain from intercourse "by mutual consent, and then only for an agreed time, to leave yourselves free for prayer", (I Cor.7,3), moralists restricted intercourse between married couples in numerous ways, but particularly on feast-days and on the night before the reception of the Eucharist. So strong has this tradition been that the question is still frequently asked by penitents whether it is lawful to go to Holy Communion if intercourse occurs after Confession and before the actual reception of the Eucharist. If one accepts the sacramentality of marriage, as every Catholic must, then it would appear that for a married couple there is no better preparation for reception of the Eucharist than their own sexual union.

'And so the unrealistic advice continued, with much small print and many learned references to the writers of past generations. It is the man's duty to ask for intercourse, we are told, and the wife's duty to grant it, for "because of her innate modesty requesting intercourse is gravely embarrassing to the woman". The equality of the partners in marriage seems to have been given very little consideration.

'The confessor formed by this kind of teaching would need to be a very mature personality if he were to escape its influence. Many would hold that the celibate confessor is by definition incapable of understanding the marital situation. Thus Dr Patrick Leahy of Ballyfermot, speaking after the publication of *Humanae Vitae* in 1968:

Dr Patrick Cremin, the theologian at Maynooth College, has accused doctors of interfering in something we know nothing about.

How can any priest say that? What knowledge could a priest possibly have about a man and woman in a bedroom unless he had experienced it himself.

You can listen to people talking for years and it still makes no difference.

You have to experience it before you become an authority on the subject. Dr Cremin has the cheek to accuse us of interfering in something we know nothing at all about (Quoted in Brian Murtough, *The Pope, the Pill, and the People,* pp.121-2).

'This lack of marriage experience in the confessor has been a frequent topic of discussion. *Prima facie* it seems rather unrealistic for a person to be laying down guidelines for human behaviour in a situation of which he has no experience whatever. It is no answer to this argument to say that a doctor doesn't need to have his own appendix removed in order to know how to remove it from his patient. No celibate can ever know—even theoretically—the emotional closeness involved in sexual cohabitation, and so his attempts to regulate it, and particularly his attempts to forbid its expression entirely in certain circumstances, must inevitably draw from the married person the comment that the celibate does not know what he is talking about.

'This is particularly true in relation to the great problem of today, family limitation. It is not uncommon for priests to recommend to their penitents certain solutions in this area which show a complete lack of understanding of the nature of married sexuality. Among such "solutions" is the suggestion that husband and wife sleep in separate rooms, or at least in separate beds. A number of false assumptions are hidden here. There is the assumption that the majority of marriages will not be seriously harmed by such separation; there is the assumption that adequate accommodation is available to allow such separation, and the entirely unwarranted assumption that such separation will not lead directly to marital infidelity. There is as well the complete insensitivity of the celibate to the reality that for many married couples their sleeping together is a more vital sign of their love than intercourse itself. In cases like this it may well be that the celibate is unconsciously pressing his own celibate way of life on married couples on the ground that it is the better way. Freud would have a revealing comment to make on the situation.

'At times in her history the Church has gone even further and positively recommended the virginal marriage. In presenting the family at Nazareth as the model of Christian marriage, the Church has seldom emphasised that the Holy Family was unique among families and not to be imitated in one of the factors that made it unique, namely its virginal character. It is only in this century that the Church has cancelled the right formerly conceded by canon law to newly-married couples—the right to refuse intercourse for six months in the hope that one of the partners might wish to enter a religious community. And right up to the present day a non-consummated marriage is *automatically* dissolved by the solemn religious profession of either of the partners— a prescription of law which shows little respect for a valid sacramental marriage. Even as late as April 1973 the Church seems to be insisting on the "brother and sister" relationship as the only acceptable form of cohabitation allowed to those involved in illicit unions. The unreality of such a situation for two normally sexed people need hardly be underlined.

'History may well be severe on the decision of Pope Pius XI in 1930 to adopt the so-called safe period almost as the official Catholic form of family limitation. We know today that the safe period as understood at the time ("the calendar method") was anything but safe, and the long line of confessors who in obedience to the Pope recommended the safe period to the penitents often found these same penitents returning very soon with stories of unwanted pregnancies. Even at the present time the grave limitations of the more sophisticated forms of safe period are unknown to many priests, many of whom continue to recommend it to their penitents as if it were one hundred per cent safe as a form of family limitation. Seldom is mention made of the fact that, apart from its inadequacy as a form of limitation, the safe period involves grave psychological problems for many couples—a matter which has been well documented by Dr John Marshall, the main Catholic protagonist of the safe period: see, for example, his telling statistics in *C.M.A.C. Bulletin*, 1969, No. 1, and his conclusion that "the great majority of couples do express their love physically during the period of abstinence and this not infrequently leads to a climax in both men and women. Their experience of trying to avoid this climax by eschewing any physical expression of love during the period of abstinence is that this has a bad effect upon their relationship. This needs to be borne in mind when counselling people who seek help about their conduct during the time of abstinence" (p.12).

'The priest who indiscriminately recommends the safe period to penitents with problems of family limitation may well be helping to break up marriages. The recent vocal support by some Irish missionary priests for the Billings method of family limitation—as yet untested in serious clinical trials—seems to us a matter of poor judgement as well as a matter of bad taste.

'The wide variation in advice given to Catholics in the wake of the encyclical *Humanae Vitae* is already well known. People have complained that within the confines of a single church building one priest can be found recommending the pill and another refusing absolution to those who are using it. The line of division is not always related to the age of the confessors concerned, and the point has frequently been made that many of the younger clergy appear to be more rigid in their interpretation of the encyclical than their older brethren. It may well be that the greater maturity produced by age, and by frank discussion with married friends, has persuaded many of the not-so-young clergy that a rigid "mortal-sin-every-time" attitude towards contraception is simply driving people away from the sacraments and sometimes out of the Church altogether.

'A number of conclusions automatically suggest themselves as a result of what has been said so far. If the Church continues with celibacy as a compulsory adjunct to the priesthood, she will have to ensure that her priests are sexually mature. We do not mean by this that they should be sexually experienced, but that they should understand and accept human sexuality as profoundly as it is possible to understand and accept sexuality without actually experiencing it. The jansenistic, sex-rejecting attitudes of the past will have to be got rid of, and the true Christian approach to sex as a gift of God will have to be taught to priests and lay-people alike. This has certainly not been done in the past. Many would go further and say that Catholic married people will never be able to get adequate marital guidance from their priests until celibacy becomes a voluntary discipline and married priests made available who can speak from the basis of their personal experience.

'Reading over the manuals of moral theology in preparation for the writing of this paper has led me to another conclusion—a conclusion which I find it impossible to escape—namely that the gross detail in which sexual topics are discussed in these manuals is far from healthy and betrays something of an obsession with sex. No other topic in Catholic moral teaching receives such microscopic attention. The reams of small print appear in many cases to achieve little more than the titillation of the reader's sexual fantasies, and it is scarcely uncharitable to suggest that—however innocent his intentions may have been at the conscious level—the writer could not but derive a certain amount of vicarious sexual satisfaction from the material that he was writing.

'A final thought: in all this moral discussion of sexuality, scarcely ever does one see any reference whatever to its character as a form of unselfish communication. It seems to be assumed all the time that husband and wife are acting solely for their own personal pleasure; because of this, abstinence is considered the better, the less selfish thing. Never is there any consideration given to the possibility that a man might want to have intercourse in order to make his wife happy, and vice versa—in which case intercourse would be better than abstinence as a normal rule. As an outsider to the marital situation, the present writer suspects that this is frequently the case, and on this unselfish aspect of marital behaviour he pins his faith on the future of marriage as a human and Christian institution. It is as an unselfish communication between man and woman that sexual union for the Christian most closely resembles its prototype—the love of Christ for His Church.'

PART II

MARRIAGE AND THE LAW

by William Duncan and James O'Reilly

1:INTRODUCTION

Family law has only recently begun to attract the attention it deserves. In the past the attitude of lawyers, politicians and the general public has been one of self-assured and complacent idealism. Irish family life has been held out as a paradigm to other nations. One result of this attitude has been that proposals to tinker with the mechanism of laws which surround the existing family institution have been looked upon by some as well-meaning but unnecessary, and by others as implying unwarranted criticism of an institution whose value is self-evident. What is needed now is a realism which, while accepting the value of family life, recognises the strains and pressures that modern life imposes on the family—a realism which is prepared constantly to reassess legal rules and remedies so that they both bolster the institution of marriage and at the same time afford protection to those who are vulnerable when marriage and family experiences conflict.

A few isolated areas of family law have been improved and particularly in the last ten years the legislature has begun to approach the reform of family law in a more self-critical mood. Some landmarks of this century which are worth noting are: The Illegitimate Children (Affiliation Orders) Act, 1930; The Legitimacy Act, 1931; The 1937 Constitution, particularly Articles 403.1º and 2º, and Articles 41 and 42; The Adoption Acts 1952 and 1964; The Married Women's Status Act, 1957; The Guardianship of Infants Act, 1964; The Succession Act, 1965; The Courts Act, 1971, ss. 18 and 19; The Marriages Act, 1972.   But the kernel of family life is marriage itself, and here legislation has been conspicuously deficient. In particular the legal remedies available on the breakdown of marriage have been allowed to fall sadly out of line with the social realities of modern Ireland. A more detailed discussion of these remedies follows, but as a general indictment of the existing law it only needs to be pointed out that the major matrimonial remedies administered by the High Court today are the same as, and derive from, the remedies which were provided by the ecclesiastical courts of the Church of Ireland prior to 1870—remedies developed in a bygone social era for a limited social class by the then established but minority Church.

Inadequacy of remedies is one great defect in our matrimonial law, another is the inaccessibility of those remedies to the great majority of Irish people. No legal aid exists in civil proceedings in this country. The cost of matrimonial proceedings in the High Court is very great. Unless either a husband or a wife is in a position to foot a heavy bill of costs, any but an exceedingly charitable solicitor or barrister would be unwilling to undertake litigation. The Free Legal Advice Centres, staffed mainly by law students, do a great deal to help but their resources are limited. The introduction of a properly administered system of free legal aid and advice on a nationwide basis is essential to ensure the equal administration of justice, and without it any reforms that are made in relation to matrimonial remedies may only benefit the relatively rich.

2: THE DISTRICT COURT

One of the worst defects in the existing sytem of matrimonial law is the absence of cheap and speedy matrimonial remedies. Matrimonial disputes often require the swift intervention of the courts. There may exist continuing cruelty, an attempt may have been made by one spouse to seize the children, or a wife may find herself suddenly without any source of income. In each of these cases the wife (or husband) requires an instant remedy. And, in the absence of legal aid, if that remedy is not also cheap it may be beyond the grasp of the great majority of married persons.

The most obvious existing forum for the provision of these swift and cheap remedies is the District Court. And yet this Court exercises only a minimal matrimonial jurisdiction and, with the limited exception of the Courts Act, 1971, no attempt has been made for nearly eighty years to widen its jurisdiction. In matrimonial matters the present District Court administers the law that was, prior to independence, administered in the old Magistrates' Courts which were common to Britain and Ireland. But the Imperial Parliament, when it broadened the matrimonial jurisdiction of the Magistrates' Courts in England and Wales towards the end of the last century, failed to do likewise for Ireland. The result is that, whereas the Magistrates' Courts in both Britain and Northern Ireland exercise a very wide matrimonial jurisdiction, granting separation maintenance and custody orders in a variety of marital breakdown situations, the District Courts in the Republic have a severely limited jurisdiction.

One of the unfortunate results of this absence of swift and cheap remedies has been that wives, who are unable to afford expensive High Court remedies and who need immediate protection, sometimes make use of the criminal law. Private prosecutions for assault are occasionally initiated by wives against their own husbands as a desperate attempt to gain protection where the civil law provides none. The result of such prosecutions may be short term protection, but in the long term the danger of molestation remains and any hope of reconciliation between husband and wife may be shattered by the wife undertaking the role of her husband's accuser. Most of these prosecutions would be unnecessary if the District Court provided a swift separation procedure which would not necessarily involve the imposition of criminal sanctions. Experience has shown that it is the civil and not the criminal law which should regulate the sphere of matrimonial breakdown.

The one true matrimonial remedy that the District Court does administer is regularly utilised, and its successful operation stands as a strong argument in favour of further increasing the jurisdiction of the District Court. The remedy is that provided under the Married Women (Maintenance in Case of Desertion) Act, 1886, as amended by the Courts Act 1971. These Acts provide a deserted wife with a ready means of applying for an order for maintenance for herself and her children against her errant husband. The District Court has power to order an amount not in excess of £15 per week for the wife and £5 per week for each dependant child below the age of sixteen. (More may be ordered by the High Court). In determining the precise amount payable in each case the District Justice will take into account the means of the husband and any means that the wife may have. In order to secure an order a wife must prove that she has been deserted and that her husband, while capable of supporting her and the children, has wilfully refused to do so. District Justices generally interpret desertion in a liberal manner. The desertion need not have run for any specific length of time. The concept of constructive desertion is also accepted, whereby if a husband treats his wife in such a way that she is forced to leave the matrimonial home, he may be regarded as having constructively deserted her.

Unfortunately a wife, though not her children, may lose her right to receive payment from her husband if she commits only one act of adultery. This seems a harsh penalty to impose upon a wife who, by virtue of her husband's desertion, may have undergone considerable strain and disorientation, while the husband himself may be involved in continuing adultery with another woman.

The enforcement of District Court orders made against deserting husbands presents serious difficulties. Under the Enforcement of Court Orders Act, 1940 a District Justice has at present two alternatives. He may levy the sum owed (together with the costs of the wife's application) by distress and sale of the husband's goods. Or he may sentence the husband to a period of imprisonment not exceeding three months. The trouble with the first method is that the husband may have no goods worth seizing or that the goods may be household goods in the possession of and needed by the deserted wife. The problem with the second method is that it secures the wife's poverty by confining her husband to the one place where he cannot possibly earn money and pay his wife maintenance.

It is probably true to say that it is impossible to devise a perfect method of enforcing maintenance debts. However, the present situation could be improved somewhat by the introduction of a system of attachment of earnings, under which the Court orders the husband's employer to pay part of his earnings directly into court. The system has been tried in other jurisdictions and, although it has not acted as a panacea, it has improved the chances of a wife securing her maintenance payments.

But the major defect in the District Court's matrimonial jurisdiction remains its narrow range. Apart from desertion, there are no other marital breakdown situations in which a District Justice may make an order. Where there has been persistent cruelty by one spouse or persistent drinking, where there has been lack of care and neglect not amounting to desertion, or where one spouse has behaved in such a way as to make life intolerable for the other, in none of these cases can the District Court make an order. And even where desertion can be proved the only order that can be made is a maintenance order in favour of a wife and children. A deserted husband has no remedy. A deserted wife who requires custody of her children has no inexpensive remedy in the District Court. What is needed therefore is comprehensive legislation giving the District Court power in broadly defined marital breakdown situations to make a variety of orders in favour of either spouse: separation orders, maintenance orders and at least temporary custody orders in relation to the children of the marriage.

3:THE HIGH COURT

The matrimonial jurisdiction of the High Court is, in the main, contained in the Matrimonial Causes and Marriage Law Ireland (Amendment) Act, 1870. The reliefs there available are specified in Section 7. Not all are relevant or appropriate on breakdown of marriage. The four reliefs mentioned are:

A. A decree of nullity
B. A decree of divorce *a mensa et toro*
C. A decree for the restitution of conjugal rights
D. A decree for jactitation of marriage

A. A decree of nullity

A decree of the Courts annulling a marriage is a most important relief in our jurisdiction as it is the only decree which allows either party mentioned to remarry during the lifetime of the other. It is important to understand the nature of this decree. A decree of nullity declares a marriage null and void. In the language of the law, this means that it never existed. So, what looked like a marriage was not a marriage because an essential prerequisite was missing, for example, both parties were within the prohibited relationships laid down by law. Accordingly, if a brother and a sister fraudulently persuade a registrar to marry them, notwithstanding the form of marriage, in the eyes of the law it is a nullity.

The grounds for a decree of nullity, briefly, are as follows:

1. Lack of capacity

Marriage is a contract and both parties must have capacity to contract. The following are the main incidents of capacity. Firstly, both parties must be of single status. This means that they must be either unmarried, or a widow or widower. A divorcee can remarry in Ireland if the degree of divorce dissolving his previous marriage is recognised here. Secondly, they must be of sufficient age. At present, the law provides that a girl can marry at twelve and a boy at fourteen. This is the old rule at common law, similar in inspiration to the age of criminal responsibility which commences at seven. Section 1 of the Marriages Act, 1972, proposes raising the marriage age to sixteen for both parties but this section is not in force yet. Thirdly, they must be outside the prohibited relationships proscribed by law. Fourthly, they must have ability to consent and lastly, they must be of different sex. Marriage of its very nature implies that there be one man and one woman. Unlike some jurisdictions, common law admits of no exceptions in this regard.

2. Certain defects in the formalities of marriage

The Marriage Acts, which stretch from 1844 to 1972, lay down the formalities that must be complied with regarding the solemnisation of marriage. These acts apply principally to non Roman Catholic marriages and include all marriages of the other religious denominations and civil marriages in the office of the registrar. The following remarks on formalities do not apply to Roman Catholic marriages, apart from those Catholics who only go through a civil ceremony. (The Roman Catholic Church is in a unique position regarding the marriage laws. As a result of an historic anomaly, they have always been outside the sphere of the Marriage Acts. The principal formality, so far as this religion is concerned, is registration of all marriages performed in catholic churches, laid down by the Registration of Marriage (Ireland) Act, 1863. This statute is of procedural rather than substantive importance.)

An example of a void marriage under this heading is where the parties wilfully intermarry without the proper publication of banns. This is provided for by the Registration of Marriages (Ireland) Act, 1844, Section 49. For example, if two Church of Ireland Protestants choose to marry by publication of banns (and not all marriages need be so solemnised in this manner) and they wilfully give their wrong names in an effort to defeat parental disapproval, a subsequent marriage will be null and void. Both parties wilfully and knowingly published their wrong names and so contravened the Marriage Acts.

3. Absence of consent

If there is no consent there is no contract, as marriage, being an agreement is based on the consent of the parties. The question the law must answer is whether the consent given in a particular case is valid. This is a difficult area of the law, as it raises questions of duress and fraud. The following remarks illustrate points considered.

A person is unable to consent to marriage if he is insane or is he is so drunk as not to know what he is doing. The problem that causes most difficulty, however, is where there has been fraud (for example, false attribution of paternity) and duress (forcing a person, against his wishes, to marry). As the law now stands, it would seem that fraud alone will not satisfy, there must also be an element of duress. An example, based on a leading Irish case, *Griffith v Griffith*

[1944] I.R. 35, best illustrates the point. The girl informs the boy that she is carrying his child. He is ignorant of the facts of life and accepts her allegation. He is told by the girl and her mother that if he doesn't marry her, he will face prosecution for unlawful carnal knowledge. (The girl was under seventeen at the date of the alleged intercourse, making it an offence under the Criminal Law Amendment Act, 1935; the consent of the girl in such cases is irrelevant.) He does not want to marry the girl. He asks his father and the local curate what he should do. Both tell him that the only option open to him is to make an honest woman of the girl concerned. In this situation, marriage is presented as his only avenue of escape. In these circumstances, he married the girl. He soon discovers that his wife is not pregnant and that, in fact, he has been tricked. When he subsequently petitioned for a decree of nullity on the grounds of duress, the Court, not surprisingly, granted the relief sought. Quite clearly, his consent to the marriage had been brought about by duress. The case is also a classic example of a 'shot gun marriage', a marriage of doubtful validity because of the pressures that may be brought to bear on the minds of the parties involved.

A difficulty that the Court at present must face is the advance made by medicine, particularly since the second world war. Psychology and psychiatry have opened up new areas where it can be suggested that a person is labouring under a personality disorder of such a nature as to make him incapable of giving what would otherwise be treated as a valid consent. In this context, for example, how do you treat the consent of a schizophrenic or a psychopath. These are areas alien to the common law. Psychic irregularities have been taken into account in recent years in the development of canon law. However, to date, civil law has not encountered a sufficient number of cases to be able to discern a possible trend.

4. *Impotence*

If either party is incapable of consumating the marriage, this may constitute a ground for relief. To be impotent in the eyes of the law, the parties must be incapable of copulating not incapable of procreating. Sterility has no relevance whatsoever to impotence and can never constitute a heading of relief. Civil law, in decided cases to date, has drawn a line between impotence (physical impediment or malformation) and wilful refusal (psychological aversion to the marriage act) to consummate a marriage. Impotence constitutes a ground of relief, wilful refusal does not. The dividing line between these instances is wafer thin and it is likely that if the matter is reviewed again (the last reported case was in 1942) the old cases will be overruled and wilful refusal will also constitute a ground.

There is an additional complicating factor here as Irish precedents have laid down that a petitioner (a party looking for a decree of nullity) cannot rely upon his own impotence. The marriage must also have been repudiated by the respondent (the party defending the suit). This rule was abolished in England in 1948 and its present application in Ireland may be doubtful.

5. Void and Voidable marriages

When talking about nullity, an essential distinction that must be drawn is that between void and voidable marriages. The first three headings above render a marriage void, the last heading (Impotence) and non-compliance with the marriage age only renders it voidable. The form of the decree, oddly enough, is the same in both cases. The vital importance of the distinction is that where a marriage is void, it will be treated by the law as never having come into existence and a decree of the Court is not needed to annul it. If a decree is granted, it is merely declaratory of an already existing state of affairs. On the other hand, where a marriage is voidable, that marriage is treated as a valid marriage, until a decree of the Courts annuls it. A decree of nullity is essential to annul a voidable marriage.

Notwithstanding the above, for the sake of certainty, a decree of nullity (where the marriage is void) is advisable. If a party remarries without getting a decree, he may be liable to prosecution for bigamy. More important, if the ground of nullity he is relying on is duress, and if this is of a highly subjective nature, a decree is most advisable. The same applies, with greater force, if he treats the consent of one party to the marriage as invalid on the grounds of some psychic irregularity. If prosecuted for bigamy, it would always be open to a person to plead that his first marriage was void. It is uncertain to what extent this plea would be successful.

6. The relationship between the nullity jurisdiction of the State and the nullity jurisdiction of the matrimonial tribunals of the Roman Catholic Church

So far as the State is concerned, there is only one jurisdiction with competence in nullity matters and that is vested in the High Court under the Matrimonial Causes and Marriage Law Ireland (Amendment) Act, 1870. Our legal system does not recognise the jurisdiction of the matrimonial tribunals of the Roman Catholic Church, nor does it recognise a decree of nullity it may grant annulling a marriage. (The Roman Catholic Church is the only religious denomination with its own matrimonial tribunals; other religious denomination in Ireland can only avail of the High Court in nullity matters.) There is a clear clash in jurisdictions here. A Roman Catholic is canonically single after a decree of nullity granted by a matrimonial tribunal yet, so far as the law is concerned, he is still legally married. If he remarries in the Church, he is liable to prosecution for bigamy.

This problem is further complicated by two factors. The first is the consequences of the development of the concept of nullity in canon law. The nullity jurisdiction of the matrimonial tribunals is a sophisticated one which has received considerable development in recent years. In comparison, the nullity jurisdiction of the civil law has been little availed of, with the result that much of its case law reflects the thinking of the nineteenth century. The last reported decision was in 1944, though two recent un- reported judgments suggest that civil law may be changing in this regard. As a result of this the grounds of nullity in canon law are considerably wider than those existing at civil law. Accordingly, a person may have his marriage annulled in canon law on grounds that are not recognised in civil law.

Clearly, that person is in a dilemma. Even if he tries to get a civil decree of nullity, he would seem bound to fail.

The second complicating factor is the question of costs. The proper course for a catholic to take after a decree of nullity has been granted in canon law is to commence proceedings for a civil decree in the High Court. This is an expensive procedure and the costs of High Court proceedings are well beyond the means of most people. Again, a catholic who has got a decree from the matrimonial tribunals of the Church is in a dilemma. In contrast, in canon law, the question of costs does not assume such importance. If the parties can afford to pay, they do, if they cannot, nothing is said. In comparison with the costs of a High Court action, proceedings in the matrimonial tribunals are very small.

This area is a complicated one but nevertheless a satisfactory solution will have to be found. The High Court has not enough power in nullity matters. The whole concept of nullity will have to be re-examined. This may entail widening the grounds of nullity, and also giving the High Court ancillary powers to deal with such questions as property and maintenance consequent on a nullity decree. From the standpoint of the Roman Catholic Church, any solution will have to take into account their jurisdiction in nullity matters.

B A decree of divorce a mensa et toro

A decree of divorce *a mensa et toro* is in effect a judicial separation. It is an order that the husband and wife shall live apart, but it does not fully dissolve the matrimonial bond and the parties are not entitled to remarry. The decree may be accompanied by an order for the payment of alimony, a periodic payment of maintenance worked out on the basis of the respective incomes of the two spouses.

The grounds on which the decree may be ordered are adultery, cruelty and unnatural offences (on the part of the husband). The reported cases in which decrees have been granted on the grounds of cruelty suggest that the petitioner must be able to prove that the respondent's behaviour was such as to endanger the petitioner's health and physical well-being. In all the successful petitions there has been some element of physical cruelty though the Court has also been prepared to consider evidence of mental cruelty. It remains to be seen whether the Court would be prepared to grant a decree in a case where no physical violence has taken place. Desertion is not a ground for divorce *a mensa et toro*. The High Court does however have power to order maintenance for a deserted wife and her children under the Courts Act, 1971.

One advantage that a wife has in bringing an action for divorce *a mensa et toro* is that her husband may be required to pay her costs even though her action is unsuccessful. She need only show that she had reasonable cause for seeking relief. But the wife's favoured position is of course conditional on her husband having sufficient substance to pay the considerable costs that would be involved in the action. The husband may also be required to pay his wife alimony during the course of the litigation which may be protracted.

The defects in the divorce *a mensa et toro* procedure are numerous and as a result very few such petitions ever come to trial. As Mr Justice Kenny has said, 'the cases involve petitions, answers, applications for alimony, settlement of issues before the Master, motions to fix the amount of security to be given by the husband and finally a jury trial lasting three or four days.' Mr Justice Kenny has given the advice to solicitors never to bring a separation action if any other method is available of procuring a reasonable financial settlement. Also the Court is very limited in the financial orders that it may make. It can award alimony, but it cannot order the payment of a lump sum or the transfer of property as between spouses. In days of rapid inflation such orders would be of great benefit to wives.

Apart from the procedural complexities the chief drawbacks of divorce *a mensa et toro* are first its costs, which in the absence of legal aid makes it an unrealistic remedy for the vast majority of Irish husbands and wives, and secondly the fact that the remedy is based on the outmoded doctrine that matrimonial remedies should only be available where a matrimonial offence can be proved. It is suggested that the proper basis for affording separation facilities should be the temporary or permanent breakdown of marriage, which may or may not be the result of specific matrimonial offences.

C Decree for Restitution of Conjugal Rights

Like a decree for jactitation, a decree for restitution of conjugal rights is very little sought after and also of very little relevance in breakdown of marriage. The last reported case was in 1959. Essentially, this decree is the law's answer for desertion. Desertion does not constitute a matrimonial offence in divorce *a mensa et toro* proceedings because our matrimonial law has never regarded it so. This is a vestige from the old ecclesiastical courts. In the eyes of the law, the relief open to either party to a marriage where there has been desertion is to petition for restitution. The court's jurisdiction is founded on residence not domicile. A good defence to a petition is either adultery or cruelty on the part of the petitioner. If the petitioner has been guilty of desertion, and is now seeking restitution, this is not a ground for refusing relief. For failure to comply with a decree, attachment would seem to be the appropriate remedy.

D Decree for Jactitation of Marriage

This action is mainly of historical interest; it is of very little practical application, the last reported decision being in 1912. A decree of jactitation prevents one party from boasting that he or she, as the case may be, is the petitioner's spouse. If granted, the decree is, in effect, an injunction preventing a named party from claiming to be married to the petitioner. The action is of very little practical importance.

4:OTHER RELIEF

A Guardianship Proceedings

The Court's jurisdiction in guardianship matters is laid down in the Guardianship of infants Act, 1964, one of the few statutes in our jurisdiction reflecting a modern and realistic approach to the family. Because of the expense of divorce *a mensa et toro* proceedings, if there are children of the marriage, the parties are more likely to take guardianship proceedings. The principal advantages are: the proceedings are less costly, both the Circuit Court and High Court have jurisdiction, proceedings must be heard in camera and the procedure is much quicker.

The court has jurisdiction in all matters concerning the welfare of children, legitimate and illegitimate. The Court has no power regarding maintenance or property in these proceedings. However, as children are the most important asset of a marriage, once their future has been determined to an extent by the court, the husband and wife are usually more agreeable to coming to some agreement on their other outstanding difficulties. For this reason, it would seem the proceedings are the most popular of all reliefs in the High Court in this sphere.

Under section 11 of the Act, where a husband or wife are unable to agree on any matter regarding the welfare of the child, either may apply to the court which may make such order as it thinks proper. A husband and wife need not be living apart to make an application under this section; under this section the Court has the following powers: (1) to give such directions as it sees fit regarding the custody of the infant and access to the infant of his father or mother and (2) order the father or the mother to pay such 'weekly or other periodical sum' for the child's maintenance that 'the court considers reasonable'. The Court has no power to award maintenance, unless the parties are living apart; if the parties are living separate, and later cohabit for a period of three months after the order, the order shall cease to have effect. It is important to note that the court can only award maintenance for the child not for the mother or father.

In granting custody, the only consideration the court takes into account is the welfare of the child. Welfare is defined in section 2 as comprising the religious and moral, intellectual, physical and social welfare of the infant. Other considerations are irrelevant. Custody of a child is not a prize for good matrimonial behaviour. It is important to distinguish custody from guardianship. All custody decides is where the child is to reside as of now. It does not take away the other parent's rights as joint guardian of the child. So, if custody of a daughter is given to the mother, any decision within the sphere of the joint guardianship of the parents must be made together, for example, the school they intend for their child or whether the child should leave the jurisdiction for any length of time. If the parties cannot agree, they must return to the Court and get its answer. An award of custody is not final; it can be varied at any time as circumstances change and as children grow up.

An example best suffices; there are three children to the marriage, a boy aged nine, a girl aged seven, and a boy aged five. Custody of the youngest child is given to the mother, as, all things being equal, it is better that younger children be with their mother. Custody of the elder boy was given to the father. He is approaching the stage where his father is starting to play a more important role in his life. The court's greatest difficulty surrounds the only girl. One High Court judge has described the decision to be made in these proceedings as 'an agonising choice', because of the many difficulties involved. In this case, the court granted custody to the father. It was felt that the comradeship that existed between the two eldest children should be maintained. Also, the girl had lived up to then in the family home (which belonged to the father) and it was thought better not to disturb this pattern. (It should be added that the father was in a position to be at home at all times and available to give his children all his attention.) The mother appealed to the Supreme Court, who by a majority of three to two, upheld the decision of the High Court.

As mentioned above, a decision of the court regarding custody is not final. In this case, the father tried to wrest the youngest son from his mother, and to this end corrupted all his children in a distasteful subterfuge. On a fresh application by the mother, for variation of the original order, the High Court gave custody of all children to the mother as the husband had so conducted himself as to render himself unfit to have custody.

The fact that a case such as this produced so many different opinions and decisions is indicative of the unenviable task any court has in these proceedings.

B Property Disputes

Disputes between a husband and wife normally concern the matrimonial home. The only sure way, a husband and wife can be certain that his or her interest in the property will be protected is to have the title to the house in joint names. If this is not the case, the party who is named in the title deeds has a considerable legal advantage. So much so, that he or she may be able to sell the house over the head of the other party to the marriage, even if there is an objection. On the other hand, if the conveyance of the property is in the joint names of the husband and wife, equality is secured. This is the only legal way at present of achieving this equality.

The property disputes the courts have to face most often are instances where the title to the home is in the husband's name. If a wife wants to prevent a husband selling the property over her head, her main relief is an application under Section 12 of the Married Women's Status Act, 1957. This section, reinacting earlier English legislation, dating from 1882, provides that in a property dispute between husband and wife concerning the possession or title to property, the court can make such order regarding title to property as it thinks fit. In theory, that sounds as if justice can be achieved, but in practice there are strings attached. The principle of separate property applies in dealings between husband and wife. Translated into reality, if a wife wants to claim an interest in the house, she must be able to point to some material contribution on her part. For example, putting down a deposit or a substantial part of it, making substantial improvements to the property (e.g. renovations or central heating). In an effort to achieve a just solution, the court may take into account money earned by a wife before she settled down to have children. So, if a wife says to the husband, that she will pay all the household bills and other household outgoings so he can concentrate on repaying the mortgage or the bank overdraft on the house, the law will be able to help her. They would look at these payments, which over a number of years would amount to a substantial sum, as entitling her to an interest in the house, should she later petition for relief.

However, the principle of separate property on which this section rests is not the best for settling these property problems. Marriage is a community which needs special rules for settling disputes concerning its assets; this it has not got. If a wife feels that her husband is about to sell, she can take out a summons under section 12 of the Act. Although the action may not be heard for some time she must make sure that her action is entered in the *lis pendens*. This is a list of pending actions and if the husband tried to sell the property before the dispute was settled, the cause of action would show up in the searches by a prospective purchaser, and the sale would fall through. Thus a wife has a way of styming her husband. She would have to satisfy herself that she has a reasonable cause of action before taking this step. If she has not (and her legal advisers will so inform her) she runs the risk of being penalised in costs. This means that if she loses her action she may have to pay the cost of her husband's solicitor and counsel, as well as her own.

This is where the law is most defective. If a wife only performs her maternal functions, in bearing children and feathering the family nest, she is in a weak position should she later look to the law for relief. She has made no material contribution to the property; she didn't work after marriage as she had a child immediately; a mother in those circumstances is extremely vulnerable under the present law and she should be protected.

The injustice outlined in the above example is all the more obvious if we look at the position of such a woman on the death of her husband. Under the provisions of the Succession Act, 1965, irrespective of what her husband's will might provide, she has a legal right to a fixed share of his assets. She can also require the dwelling house to be appropriated as part of her legal right share. (This does not apply to a farm house or guest house used also as a dwelling house.) In short, the law guarantees her certain rights

70

because she is a married woman. The provision of the Succession Act applies equally to husbands and wives.

C Miscellaneous Relief

There are a number of miscellaneous reliefs that the law provides for the loss of consortium in marriage. Consortium has never been exactly defined but includes that bundle of rights that a husband has in his wife and a wife has in her husband. Both parties are entitled to each other's society, and if anyone interferes with this, or if either is deprived of the consortium of the other, there are possible legal remedies. Sexual relations are a facet of consortium.

(i) Damages for loss of consortium and services

If a husband is wrongfully deprived of his wife's consortium by the wrongdoing of another, he has a cause of action against that person. He can only recover for total loss, not the partial loss, of his wife's consortium. For example, if a wife is injured as a result of a certain person's negligence in a car crash, apart altogether from his wife's claim in negligence, the husband has a cause of action against that person for the loss of consortium of his wife. This could arise where the wife has to spend a considerable time in hospital. Only the husband has a right to claim under this heading; a wife cannot claim in similar circumstances. The survival of this action is anomalous and based on the same principle as the succeeding case.

(ii) An action for Criminal Conversation

Like the immediately preceding remedy, this one is also available to a husband. It is available by a husband against anyone who commits adultery with his wife. Criminal conversation means adultery. The fact that the wife has consented is irrelevant. The action is normally tried by a jury who decide the monetary compensation to which the husband is entitled. In assessing damages, there are two headings the jury consider, firstly, the pecuniary aspect and secondly the consortium aspect.

Under the first heading (the pecuniary aspect) the jury assess the value of the wife. Considerations that have been taken into account by the Courts include the wife's fortune, her assistance in her husband's business, her capacity as a housekeeper and her ability generally in the home.

Under the second heading (the consortium aspect) the court is to assess the proper compensation to the husband for this blow to his marital honour and the embarrassment and injury to his sense of probity and family pride. The damages will depend upon the purity and general character of his wife. In the words of an early report, if the wife be of 'wanton disposition or disloyal instincts', the husband's loss is small as her value to him is so much the less. If, on the other hand, she was guiled by the 'assiduous seduction' and 'practiced artifice' of a seducer, then, obviously, her value to him is much greater.

The action is anomalous, and like that for damages for loss of consortium is based on the old common law concept that the husband's interest in his wife is a quasi-proprietary one. They are both vestiges from past days and have no relevance in modern society. These proceedings, if they are commenced in our jurisdiction, are heard in open court. This is undesirable because of the unsavoury publicity given to such cases. Like other family matters, these should be heard in camera. Two recent cases in Ireland where substantial damages were awarded make repeal of this action all the more desirable.

A husband may also get damages against a person for harbouring his wife and for enticement. Enticement is the only relief where the wife has an equal claim for relief.

(iii) Damages for Death

This is the most common and is provided for by the Fatal Accidents Acts and The Civil Liability Acts 1962 and 1964. The most usual source of these actions are automobile crashes. The newspapers are full of such examples.

5:SOCIAL WELFARE LEGISLATION

Until recently social welfare legislation made no specific provision for wives who were suffering financial hardship as a result of a broken marriage. In the absence of other grounds for social assistance such wives were thrown back on Home Assistance.

In Section 22 of the Social Welfare Act, 1970 the legislature admitted for the first time the principle of the State's responsibility to provide financial support in a marital breakdown situation. The wives who were picked out for this special treatment were those who had been deserted. The Deserted Wife's Allowance scheme came into operation on 1 October, 1970, and three years later about 3,000 wives with dependent children were benefitting under the scheme.

The Deserted Wife's Allowance is available to wives who are unable to secure and enforce maintenance orders against their husbands. Before a wife may become entitled to an allowance she must be able to show that 'she has made and continues to make reasonable efforts within the means available to her to trace her husband's whereabouts and to prevail on him to resume living with her or to contribute to the support and maintenance of her and her children'. Proof of desertion does not of itself entitle a wife to the allowance. Unless she is over forty years of age, the deserted wife must have one or more dependent children. The wife must be able to prove that the desertion has continued for a period of at least six months, and any substantial contributions by the husband towards his wife's maintenance, even though sporadic, may be fatal to the wife's claim for an allowance. The wife must also satisfy a stringent means test.

There are indications that the Department of Social Welfare, after an initial period during which rules were applied somewhat inflexibly, has begun to administer the scheme in a more liberal manner. The rule that the husband must 'of his own volition' have left the wife is not rigorously applied. If for example a wife has secured a District Court maintenance order against her husband on the basis of *constructive* desertion (i.e. where, because of the husband's conduct, the wife has left him) this may be accepted by the Department as sufficient evidence of desertion. The fact that a husband has made small and irregular payments to his wife will not necessarily extinguish the wife's right to an allowance. And, where a husband has secured a foreign divorce decree, that decree will not now automatically bar the wife's right to an allowance.

In July 1973 a new Deserted Wife's Benefit was introduced to assist deserted wives whose own or whose husband's insurance under the Social Welfare Acts meets the required standard. Such wives are now entitled to a Benefit which has the great advantage of being free of a means test. Income from employment or any other source does not affect the wife's right to the new Benefit. The Deserted Wife's Allowance, which is means tested, continues to be payable to the deserted wife who does not qualify for the new Benefit.

The legislation which has been passed over the last three years is clearly welcome, but it is doubtful whether it has gone far enough. Apart from specific criticisms concerning the amount of Allowance or Benefit involved, the existence of a stringent means test in relation to the Allowance and difficulties over the definition of desertion, there is the more general criticism that the legislature was wrong to provide social welfare assistance in just one 'failure to maintain' situation. What, for example, of the case where a husband, though not technically in desertion, squanders his income on drink and gambling and leaves his wife and children an inadequate amount for their support? The wife in these circumstances has equal, and sometimes even greater, financial problems than the wife who has been completely deserted. The answer may be the provision by the State of an adequate allowance for the support of a wife and her children in any circumstance in which support has been withheld by the husband. It would no doubt be argued that such a scheme would amount to a State subsidy for irresponsible husbands. The answer to this may be that the State, rather than the disadvantaged wife, should shoulder the responsibility of recovering from the husband monies paid by way of allowance to the wife.

It should also be noted that there exists no deserted husband's allowance. The principle to joint parental responsibility, which is now a firmly established part of Irish Guardianship law, would seem to require that either spouse be entitled to social aid where the behaviour of the other spouse has resulted in an unbearable financial burden in bringing up the children.

6:FOREIGN LAW

The absence of facilities for full divorce in the Irish Republic sometimes results in Irish spouses seeking foreign divorces especially in England. The extent to which such divorces will be recognised in the Republic is still, owing to an ambiguous clause in the Constitution a matter of some doubt. In a recent case the High Court decided that it would recognise, for succession purposes, an English divorce granted to a couple who were domiciled in England. Thus it was held that a subsequent marriage entered into by the husband was valid and his second wife was entitled to benefits given to a wife by the Succession Act, 1965. It seems likely that this principle of recognition would be extended to areas other than succession, e.g. in questions relating to the legitimacy of children, or liability to taxation, foreign divorces probably would be recognised provided that the divorced couple were domiciled in the country where the divorce was granted. But it must be stressed that the acquisition of a foreign domicile by an Irish couple is no easy matter. The husband must be able to show that his intention was to remain permanently in the foreign country at the time of his divorce petition. Mere residence in the foreign country will probably not suffice. And a wife may still not acquire a domicile independently of her own husband.

Another vital problem concerning foreign law is that of the enforcement abroad of maintenance orders made by Irish courts. This problem generally arises where the husband has deserted his wife and has taken up employment abroad, usually in England. At the moment there exist no facilities for the mutual enforcement of maintenance orders as between the United Kingdom and the Republic. There does exist an E.E.C. Convention concerning the enforcement of civil judgments in general throughout the E.E.C. But the negotiations to adapt the Convention to the legal system of the new member states are still pending and the Convention will have no force in England or Ireland until their successful conclusion. Meantime the deserted wife must wait. Not unnaturally this situation, which the legislature has been aware of for a considerable number of years has been widely condemned and it is difficult to see why the present and past Governments could not have pursued more vigorously their attempts to conclude a convention with the United Kingdom pending the coming into force of the E.E.C. Convention.

PART III

CONCLUSION

CONCLUSION

The reason I have only very superficially referred to the legal aspects of the different cases quoted is because law specialists James O'Reilly and William Duncan have covered all the ground very adequately and professionally in their contribution on Law and Marriage.

But, the reason I have not dealt with the agencies for rehabilitating or supporting the parties in marriage conflict situations is because the structures at present are almost non-existent, and consequently ineffective.

Very obviously, our society has not realistically accepted the prevailing trend of marital breakdown and broken families in Ireland. Therefore, it has not seen fit to spend money on a social problem that technically does not exist. We have a woefully stunted framework of social care, I know, for I have tried to pull the bits and pieces together so many times, it's like making a jigsaw puzzle with half the shapes missing.

At the time of writing, we have no State administered citizens advice bureaux or information centres, no free legal aid in civil cases, home help only in extreme circumstances. The country's social problems are in the hands of no more than 80 overworked social workers, many of whom confess that they cannot aspire to do casework, at best they can keep a tenuous contact with the most pressing cases, but can do no preventative or follow-up work. Catering for general community health, child care etc we have 770 Public Health nurses, covering the whole population, which compares very unfavourably with other European countries. Finland, for instance, the poorest of the Scandinavian countries, with a standard of living not so different from our own, has 3,300 Public Health nurses.

One area where the Churches have in recent years taken the initiative and attempted to help the marriages in distress, is with Marriage Counselling. Already centres exist in every diocese, and at the Catholic Marriage Counselling centre in Dublin, so great is the demand for the service that there is a four week delay to get a first appointment. But is marriage counselling affiliated as it is to specific religions, the answer to the problem, or is it merely a manipulative service with vested interests?

Undoubtedly, the personnel who operate the counselling services for both the Catholic Church and the Church or Ireland are very worthy people, but they must work, both within the confines of the legal and social structures that exist, and counsel within the often inflexible doctrine of their churches.

In the cases with which I have been involved, and I accept that I only become involved when there is pathetically little left of the original relationship, I have found that marriage counselling has either been rejected out of hand by the spouse, or else tried and found inadequate. As an immediate medium of advice or assistance, it was found less than effective, which in view of the nature of counselling is not surprising. It involves not so much the problem, as the person in relation to that problem, and it entails the gradual establishment of a relationship between the client and the professional counsellor, the rapport so essential to the casework being built up by a series of weekly dialogues. Marriage Counsellors themselves freely admit the restrictions of the service, some see it as a middle class exercise for middle class people with marriage problems. They say they are not getting to the hardcore of the problem cases. In rural areas the people who most need the help are reluctant to seek it, and at all centres it is an established fact that it is wives, but seldom husbands who come. Undoubtedly, marriage counselling could be more effective, if the backing-up agencies and the social help structures were available to complement the worthy involvement in counselling.

As I mentioned at the beginning this book does not purport to be a statistical study of the position of women in Irish marriages, neither does it pretend to be a sociological study into the subject. But I hope it presents a picture of the type of situations many Irishwomen find themselves in by marriage tradition, custom and law in our country. Some points are worth recording, even obvious ones like the fact that a woman becomes a financial cripple when she becomes a mother, she needs protection, support and an understanding that should match the priceless job she is doing. Her status in this country as of now is unjustifiable.

On the question of education, virtually everyone who has gone through the Irish educational system has been emotionally stunted by our repressive attitudes to sex. The number of problem marriages where this has had an effect for the worse is impossible to assess, but psychologists and social workers alike feel many of the situations I have discussed, like excessive drinking, brutality, infidelity, impotence could be linked with early conditioning that portrayed sex as sinful. There is a great deal of talk if not action on the need for education of adolescents for marriage, and while this could be a welcome innovation, the sad fact is that a happy home is the best school, and the overriding question is clearly how to stop the self-perpetuation of the broken homes.

Some danger points can be seen for what they are, like the strong inevitability of the shotgun marriage ending in disaster, many of today's deserted wives were yesterday's pregnant brides. Another obvious area of stress, and one that should be avoidable, is overcrowding in living accommodation, the young couples unable to afford a home, or the stress of doubling-up and living with in-laws.

According to Jack Dominion, author of *Marital Breakdown*, trouble can develop because of a couple's inability to establish a mutually satisfying and strong relationship at the first stage of marriage. This is called the 'honeymoon period', and lasts until the birth of the first child. In Ireland this can approximate in many cases to about nine months and two weeks, hardly long enough one would imagine for a couple to put down roots for this mutually satisfying relationship that will meet the emotional and social needs of each other for life. To say that marriage is changing because the concept of woman's role in today's world is changing may appear to be oversimplifying a complex situation, but what is indisputable however is the apparent change in the stress points of many women. No longer will the traditional idea that marriage is a vocation that must be suffered through, be accepted by Irish wives. And there is welcome evidence of a greater understanding and toleration of the

81

separated parent, which in turn is reducing the sense of stigma so many have had to suffer with in the past.

It is neither an original nor a profound ending to say that there are no guarantees with marriage, but I feel strongly that until Irishwomen are prepared to critically examine their reasons for getting married, the rights they forfeit in marriage, and the reality and consequences of marital breakdown, they will continue to be the unequal and disadvantaged partners in their marriages.

Nuala Fennell   January 1974.

APPENDIX

Headquarters of semi-State and Voluntary Organisations involved in community support for the family.

Al-anon—The Country Shop, 23 St Stephen's Green, Dublin.
Alcoholics Anonymous—26 Essex Quay, Dublin 8.
Association of Irish Widows—3 North Earl St, Dublin 1.
A.D.A.P.T. (Association for Deserted Parents) P.O. Box 673, Dublin 3.
Ally—Dominican Priory, Dorset St, Dublin 1
Cherish (Association for the Unmarried Mother) 335 Lr. Kimmage Rd, Dublin 6.
Catholic Marriage Advisory Council—35 Harcourt St. Dublin 2
Church of Ireland Marriage Advisory Centre—39 Molesworth St, Dublin 2.
Free Legal Aid Centres (F.L.A.C.)—Ozanam House, 53 Mountjoy Sq. Dublin 1.
Irish National Council on Alcoholism—19 Fleet St, Dublin.
Irish Society for the Prevention of Cruelty to Children—20 Molesworth St, Dublin 2.
Samaritans—66 South William St, Dublin (778833)
Salvation Army—13 Lr Abbey St, Dublin 1.
Society of St Vincent de Paul—Nicholas St, Dublin 8.